# BRIGHT NOTES

# SIDDHARTHA BY HERMANN HESSE

**Intelligent Education**

Nashville, Tennessee

BRIGHT NOTES: Siddhartha
www.BrightNotes.com

No part of this publication may be used or reproduced in any manner whatsoever without written permission, except in the case of brief quotations in critical articles and reviews. For permissions, contact Influence Publishers http://www.influencepublishers.com.

ISBN: 978-1-645422-16-7 (Paperback)
ISBN: 978-1-645422-17-4 (eBook)

Published in accordance with the U.S. Copyright Office Orphan Works and Mass Digitization report of the register of copyrights, June 2015.

Originally published by Monarch Press.
Jerry Glenn, 1973
2020 Edition published by Influence Publishers.

Interior design by Lapiz Digital Services. Cover Design by Thinkpen Designs.

Printed in the United States of America.

Library of Congress Cataloging-in-Publication Data forthcoming.
Names: Intelligent Education
Title: BRIGHT NOTES: Siddhartha
Subject: STU004000 STUDY AIDS / Book Notes

# CONTENTS

| | | |
|---|---|---|
| 1) | Introduction to Hermann Hesse | 1 |
| 2) | Composition, Publication, and Translation of Siddhartha | 18 |
| 3) | Textual Analysis | 41 |
| | Chapter One: The Son of The Brahman | 41 |
| | Chapter Two: With The Samanas | 44 |
| | Chapter Three: Gotama | 47 |
| | Chapter Four: Awakening | 50 |
| | Chapter Five: Kamala | 52 |
| | Chapter Six: With The Child-People | 55 |
| | Chapter Seven: Sansara | 58 |
| | Chapter Eight: By The River | 60 |
| | Chapter Nine: The Ferryman | 63 |
| | Chapter Ten: The Son | 66 |
| | Chapter Eleven: Om | 68 |
| | Chapter Twelve: Govinda | 70 |
| 4) | Character Analyses | 74 |
| 5) | Essay Questions and Model Answers | 83 |

6) Bibliography 88

7) Topics for Research and Criticism 100

# INTRODUCTION TO HERMANN HESSE

## FAMILY BACKGROUND

Like many German writers, Hermann Hesse came from a family which had for many generations been associated with the Protestant clergy. The father, Johannes Hesse, was a protestant clergyman who belonged to the pietistic tradition, a liberal branch of German Protestantism which stressed a concern for the individual's relationship to God above strict formal dogma. Hermann was later to acknowledge the importance of the religious atmosphere of his childhood, as, for example, in a letter dated 1950 in which he spoke of Christianity as it was lived, rather than preached, in his home. Johannes Hesse spent the years 1869 to 1873 as a missionary in India. There he acquired an interest in Oriental philosophy and theology which he was to retain for the rest of his life. Forced to return to Europe on account of poor health, he settled in Calw, a town in Southwestern Germany, where he was active as an author of works on religious subjects. Hermann's mother, Marie, came from a similar background; she had been in India as the wife of a missionary. She was living in Calw after the death of her first husband when she met Johannes Hesse.

Hermann, the second of six children, was born in Calw on July 2nd 1877. Four years later the family moved to Basel,

Switzerland, and acquired Swiss citizenship. The father continued his religious work in Basel where he became the editor of a missionary magazine. In 1886 the family returned to Calw where Hesse was to remain until leaving home to attend a boarding school in 1890. Hermann's early childhood years were for the most part pleasant and they were certainly intellectually stimulating. Literature, philosophy, and the arts were discussed and respected in his home. Guests, many of whom came from foreign lands, were often entertained there. Hermann felt an especial affinity to his mother whose loving care provided him with a feeling of security and well-being. His father, on the other hand, in spite of his tolerance in regard to many theological matters, believed in strict discipline and followed rigid theories of education which allowed no room for freedom of expression on his son's part. Many of the difficulties of these early years are reflected in Hesse's works, as, for example, in "A Child's Heart." As a boy, Hermann was not an outstanding pupil and did not enjoy school; he once remarked that he had had only one teacher whom he admired.

## SEARCH FOR A CAREER

As was common in Germany at that time, Hermann was sent to a boarding school to prepare for the difficult examination which all students had to pass in order to be admitted to advanced schools and the university. He entered the school in Göppingen in 1890 to undertake this preparation. At this school, for the only time in his life, he was an exceptionally good student. After successfully passing the examination, he followed the wishes of his father and enrolled in the famous school at Maulbronn with the intention of becoming a Protestant minister. The atmosphere of the school soon proved too oppressive and Hermann ran away. He returned, but once more was unable to adjust and soon left the school permanently. The months which followed were exceedingly traumatic for the disturbed youth. Help was sought from various persons and institutions, but Hermann's emotional problems could not be alleviated. Once he even went so far as to attempt suicide. His final exposure to formal education was at a preparatory school in Bad Cannstatt in 1893 and 1894. Hesse was not at all happy there and his experiences formed the basis for the descriptions of some of Sinclair's unhappy school experiences in *Demian*.

While doing mechanical work in a Calw clock factory in 1894 and 1895, the young Hesse decided that he wanted to become a writer. He soon found employment in a bookstore in Tübingen and began to see meaning, or at least potential meaning, in life. In 1899 he published his first books, a collection of poetry and one of short prose pieces. In that same year he moved to Basel where he continued to work in the book trade and to expand his horizons, by reading books of many different kinds, and by traveling in Switzerland and Italy. Two years later he wrote a book which attracted the attention of some important German critics and which accordingly established Hesse's reputation as an author: *The Posthumous Papers and Poems of Hermann Lauscher*.

## IMPORTANT EARLY WRITINGS

Other books followed, including, in 1904, the novel *Peter Camenzind*. This book was immediately successful and the royalties from it and from other writings gave Hesse a degree of financial independence. He was accordingly able to leave the book trade and devote himself entirely to his writing. The novel is about a poor but talented Swiss boy who grows up in harmony with nature, but decides to go out into the world where he eventually attains a measure of material success in society. He ultimately comes to realize that he has not found self-fulfillment in love, intellectual pursuits, art, music, or material goods. Following the death of his close friend Boppi, a cripple, he finally retires to lead an isolated life free of the demands of society. Already in the first of Hesse's novels we see very clearly the **theme** that will pervade all of the later ones: the difficult search on the part of an individual for identity and fulfillment.

Hesse soon became a respected member of the German literary elite and contributed stories, poems, reviews, and essays to many of the leading periodicals of that time. He also continued to write novels and the next one, *Beneath the Wheel* (1906), was to a great extent autobiographical. It relates the unsuccessful attempt of the hero, Hans Giebenrath, to cope with the stifling atmosphere of the educational system. The two sides of Hesse's own nature are shown in Hans and in Hermann Heilner, who rebelled against the system and ran away. Hans, like Hesse, experienced many disappointments and eventually found himself unable to cope with the demands of his father and of the school. In two very important respects, however, the novel does not follow Hesse's biography; Hans' mother dies when he is very young, depriving him of a source of warmth and love, and Hans himself, in a state of depression, drowns while still a young man. One of many German literary works of the early twentieth century which attacked the educational system, *Beneath the Wheel* was very popular.

Hesse's next two novels, *Gertrude* (1910) and *Rosshalde* (1914), deal with the problems of the artist. The former is one of the least autobiographical of Hesse's works. The hero, Kuhn, is a musician who enjoyed a happy childhood. He injures his leg in an accident and becomes introverted. He falls in love with Gertrude, but lacks the self-assurance to reveal his feelings to her and try to win her love. She marries another man, but the marriage is not successful and her husband commits suicide. Kuhn becomes a great composer, although he remains a lonely and unhappy person. He has limited contact with Gertrude in his later years, although she continues to be a source of inspiration for his great works of art.

## YEARS OF CRISIS

In 1904, Hesse married Maria Bernoulli, a Swiss woman nine years his elder. The couple led an isolated life in Gaienhofen. Sons were born in 1905 and 1909. Hesse was a successful and highly productive writer, but his marriage became progressively less happy. In 1911 he made a journey to the Orient in the company of the painter Hans Sturzenegger. Hesse was particularly interested in India, the country in which both of his parents had lived and which his father and grandfather had studied extensively. The trip, however, did not enable Hesse to find the peace and fulfillment which he so desperately sought. Some of his impressions are recorded in *From India* (1913). His personal conflicts are reflected rather directly in the novel *Rosshalde* (1914), the story of the painter Johann Veraguth, who lives a lonely and unhappy life at his estate, Rosshalde, with his wife and a younger son, Pierre. An older son, Albert, is away at school and returns only during vacation periods. Life acquires meaning for Veraguth through his work as an artist and his love for Pierre. He tolerates his marriage only for the sake of Pierre. What remains of his happiness is shattered when Pierre dies of meningitis. The end of the novel remains open. Veraguth, turning his back on bourgeois society, leaves Rosshalde and his wife to travel. His future is uncertain.

The outbreak of World War I in 1914 marked another crisis in Hesse's complicated personal life. Although he had been living in Switzerland for many years, he was German and his reading public expected him to support the German cause. (Switzerland remained neutral during the war.) Hesse did not immediately assume an anti-German stand, but he publicly questioned the excessive patriotism in his native country which was brought out by the war and he was in turn sharply criticized from many sides in Germany. He remained in Switzerland throughout the war and was active in the effort to improve the lot of German prisoners of war and internees.

Hesse's literary productivity continued undiminished during the first years of the war and *Knulp*, one of the more popular of his earlier works, appeared in 1915. The three stories contained in the collection will be analyzed in detail in this study guide.

The following year, 1916, was to bring severe misfortune: the death of his father, the serious illness of his son Martin, and the mental breakdown of his wife, who had to be sent to an institution. This was in fact the end of Hesse's first marriage, although he did not obtain a formal divorce until 1923. Hesse was naturally despondent and his search for psychiatric help brought him in contact with Dr. Joseph Lang, a disciple of the eminent psychologist Carl Gustav Jung. From Doctor Lang, Hesse not only received advice which helped him overcome his own personal crisis, but he also learned in detail the theories of Jung. Hesse became a devoted student of Jung and the influence of this psychologist was to become one of the most important factors in his later works.

## THE MIDDLE YEARS

*Demian* was written during a short period of time in 1917 under the immediate influence of Doctor Lang and, through him, of Jung. This new novel marks a radical break in Hesse's literary development and the author did not want his readers in any way to be reminded of his earlier works or to associate the new Hesse - the Hesse of *Demian* - with them. Accordingly he published the novel in 1919 under the pseudonym Emil Sinclair, the name of one of the main characters of the book. The novel was an immediate success. The young postwar generation felt a strong affinity to this strange, powerful work, and it was also well-received by literary critics. The Fontane Prize, a prestigious literary prize awarded for outstanding first novels, was presented to the mysterious Emil Sinclair. The prize was returned by the publisher and in 1920 Hesse revealed that he was actually the author. But he had achieved his goal. To the reading public, Hermann Hesse was now primarily known as the author of *Demian*, not of *Peter Camenzind*, *Rosshalde*, and other early works which Hesse had come to consider to be immature.

The most important **theme** of *Demian* is the necessity of first recognizing, and then integrating into one's personality, the two different aspects of life - the "light" and the "dark," the spiritual and the sensual, saintliness and sin. The setting, plot, and style of *Demian* are for the most part dissimilar from those of Hesse's previous works. It is set in Germany during the early years of the present century and describes the outer and inner development of Emil Sinclair from late childhood to maturity. Here, as in *Siddhartha, Narcissus and Goldmund*, and many of Hesse's works - although not in the stories discussed in this study guide - three distinct stages of development can be seen: the early period of innocence, a middle period which is not without searching, loneliness, and even despair, and the final period in which a synthesis is effected. When Emil Sinclair is first introduced to the "dark" world, he sees no way to reconcile the warm, serene atmosphere of his home with the cold frightening world he now sees. But with the help of Max Demian he gradually becomes more and more able to see the possibility of accepting both aspects of his human nature and he eventually finds he is no longer forced to view them as polar opposites.

The year 1919 was indeed an important one. Hesse wrote several important essays during that year, including "Zarathustra's Return" in which his debt to Nietzsche is acknowledged, and three of his better short stories, "A Child's Heart," "Klingsor's Last Summer" and "Klein and Wagner," published together in 1920 under the title *Klingsor's Last Summer*. These three stories will be analyzed in detail in this study guide. Furthermore, Hesse moved from Bern, where he had been living, to the small Swiss town of Montagnola, which was to be his home in his later years. It was also at about this time that Hesse first took up painting; he later became an accomplished painter and it was to remain his favorite hobby throughout his life. And finally, work on the next important book, *Siddhartha*, was begun in this year.

*Siddhartha* proved to be an especially difficult book to write. As Hesse remarked, the first two periods of the hero's life, those of innocence and searching, were easy for him to portray. But the final triumphant vision of the old Siddhartha was foreign to Hesse's experience and hence he had great difficulty putting it on paper. Only in 1922 was the completed novel published.

In this highly poetic book set in ancient India Hesse describes the life of Siddhartha. First the hero masters his intellect and will, and then he turns to the world of the senses. He finds neither asceticism nor hedonism totally satisfying. Late in life he finds fulfillment in a mystical vision at, and with the help of, a river, the symbol of perfection, unity, and continuity.

In 1923 Hesse became a Swiss citizen. His personal life, however, remained unsettled. He obtained a divorce from his first wife and soon thereafter (in January, 1924) he married Ruth Wenger. Five years were to lapse before the publication of his next major novel, *Steppenwolf* (1927). These years were far from totally barren. Hesse continued to publish poems, short stories, essays, and reviews in various journals and newspapers. But a feeling of alienation, which is reflected in the suffering of Harry Haller in *Steppenwolf*, continued to affect him. His second marriage, like the first, did not prove to be successful; it ended in divorce in 1927. By this time Hesse was one of the most famous writers of his generation and his first full-length biography, by Hugo Ball, appeared in conjunction with his fiftieth birthday in that same year.

*Steppenwolf*, like *Demian*, "Klein and Wagner," and "Klingsor's Last Summer," has a "realistic" setting in the twentieth century. The hero, Harry Haller, is a middle-aged man who is torn between the world of the bourgeoisie and that of the artist-intellectual. At first he believes that there are but two aspects of his personality, and that he is torn between these irreconcilable poles. He finds a mysterious "treatise" (reflecting insights of his own unconscious) which points out that his conception of a simple duality within himself was incorrect. There are not two Harry Hallers, the Steppenwolf and the bourgeois citizen, but many very different aspects of a complicated individual. Haller gradually comes to realize and accept this fact on a conscious level during the remainder of the novel, and the closing scene, the so-called "Magic Theater," symbolically represents the progress which he has made.

In 1930 one of Hesse's most popular novels appeared, *Narcissus and Goldmund*. Set in the Middle Ages (although not in any specific century), with a plot rich in adventure, the novel examines the duality of spirit and nature, incorporated by the two leading characters, Narcissus and Goldmund, respectively.

Most of the story is devoted to Goldmund's wanderings. Originally a seminarian, he is told by his friend and teacher Narcissus that he is not destined for the priesthood. He leaves the seminary and has many adventures. He has brief, but meaningful, affairs with many women; he experiences birth and death, and is himself forced to kill another human being; and great effort he becomes a skilled sculptor and produces a few pieces of extraordinary beauty. Narcissus, on the other hand, becomes a priest and intellectual. Each respects the other, and Narcissus often helps his friend in one way or another. Although Goldmund dies a realistic and un-idealized death, his way of life, which includes both the spirit and the senses, is presented as superior to that of Narcissus, whose philosophy attempts to deny death, and who, as a result, will not be able to face death when it comes, as it inevitably must. In many respects this novel invites comparison with *Knulp*.

Hesse married again in 1931. His third wife, with whom he was to remain until his death some thirty years later, was Ninon Auslander Dolbin. Hesse's happiness during these years is portrayed symbolically in the highly autobiographical, but equally unrealistic, novel *Journey to the East* (1932). The hero is named "H.H.," an obvious **allusion** to Hermann Hesse, and many other references to the author's life can be detected in the book. Once again the hero goes through three stages in his development. He naively and confidently joins a secret Order or League and takes part in its "Journey to the East." He later drops out of the League and experiences intense loneliness and despair. With the help of Andreas Leo, a figure who resembles the old Siddhartha in some respects, he finally comes to understand the League, and himself, and then comes to feel a sense of harmony with the world.

For Hesse, unlike most important German-speaking writers, Hitler's rise to power in the early 1930s did not signal any radical changes. Hesse was already a Swiss citizen and although his hatred of war - and of the other things for which Nazism stood- remained undiminished, he was not and never had been a political activist. He had little faith in practical politics and hence did not join the active political opposition to the Nazis. In the early 1930s, under the dark cloud which covered Europe, Hesse began work on his last great novel, *The Glass Bead Game*, or *Magister Ludi*, as it is often called in English. According to Hesse's original plans, this work was to consist of a number of "autobiographies" which would describe successive reincarnations of a single person. Hesse's conception of the novel changed as he was writing it and the emphasis shifted to the final historical period, the world of Castalia, about the year 2400 A.D. The three autobiographies of Joseph Knecht that are appended to the novel are vestiges of the original plan, and a fourth autobiography was also written but not included in the book. As Hesse himself later stated, the writing of *The Glass Bead Game* was his own spiritual defense against the deadly political and moral climate in the world at that time.

Joseph Knecht's biographies and poems, which are appended to the narrator's dry, pedantic biography, most clearly reveal the novel's important issues and themes. Knecht comes to realize that he must seek oneness with nature, but is not able to formulate his ideas, let alone express them adequately and directly in words. He ultimately does realize that he cannot find what he is seeking in the rarified atmosphere of Castalia, and accordingly forsakes it in favor of a life in the "real" world. He dies before coming to a full conscious realization of the significance of his feelings and actions, and critics hence sometimes debate the validity of his life. But he has remained true to himself, and his life must therefore be called successful.

## OLD AGE

Hesse's reputation continued to grow after the publication of *The Glass Bead Game*. He was awarded the Nobel Prize for literature - the world's highest literary award-in 1946, and later received several other important prizes and awards in recognition of his literary work. He continued to write poetry and short prose pieces and he faithfully answered the numerous letters addressed to him by admiring readers, although he felt uncomfortable in the role of advisor and father confessor. But *The Glass Bead Game* was to be his last novel. As the years went by, he guarded his privacy more and more carefully and seldom left his secluded home at Montagnola, of which he was so fond. He died of a brain hemorrhage on August 9, 1962, a month after his eighty-fifth birthday.

## INTELLECTUAL INFLUENCES

It would be impossible even to list all of the important influences on Hesse. He was exposed to theology, philosophy, literature, and the other arts at an early age and retained his varied interests throughout his long life. Among the literary figures whom he most admired, however, two deserve particular mention: the mystical Romantic poet Novalis (pseudonym of Friedrich von Hardenberg, 1772-1801), and Johann Wolfgang von Goethe (1749-1832), about whom Hesse once said: "Among all German writers, Goethe is the one to whom I owe the most, the one to whom I am most deeply indebted, who has held my attention, enslaved and encouraged me, forced me to follow his lead or vigorously attack it." Hesse also knew many religious and philosophical writers. As was mentioned above, Christianity was quite important as a formative influence. He also studied various Eastern religions in some depth.

Two of the most important influences on Hesse's thought must be discussed here: the philosopher and poet Friedrich Nietzsche (1844-1900) and the psychologist Carl Gustav Jung (1875-1961). Before going into the extent of these influences, however, it must be emphasized that individuality remained one of Hesse's fundamental values. He read Nietzsche and Jung, as well as Goethe, Novalis, Dostoevski, Freud, and other great writers, but always with a critical eye. Although Hesse did not imitate Nietzsche, Jung, or anyone else, an understanding of certain basic concepts of Nietzsche and Jung can facilitate the approach to some of Hesse's difficult works.

Nietzsche and Jung share some important beliefs which are also to be found in the works of Hesse. Perhaps the most important of these is the insistence upon the necessity of finding one's own path toward self-realization, and of accepting the dark, so-called "sinful" side of human nature in the process. Nietzsche called for a complete revaluation of moral standards entirely eliminating the Judeo-Christian morality which he felt represented a philosophy that valued weakness and conformity rather than strength and individuality, which he preferred. Hesse, too, continually rejects weakness and conformity. The concept which Nietzsche called amor fati ("Love of fate") is likewise shared by Hesse. This concept refers to a joyful acceptance of the world as it is; it is a highly affirmative philosophy, and variations of it can be seen in Klingsor and Klein.

Jung, in more practical terms, refers to the inferior, animalistic side of our nature as the "shadow," and warns against the bad effects of simply attempting to repress it. This part of our human nature must rather be first understood, and then accepted, he maintains. Other of Jung's concepts are also useful in understanding Hesse, especially those of the "unconscious" and the "archetype." Jung believes that a large body of experiences remain in a person's unconscious (he objects to Freud's term "subconscious," which seems to him to carry derogatory implications). Each individual has elements which are part of his "personal unconscious"; that is, memories and emotions from his past which have been removed from his immediate conscious memory, but which may still exert an important and even decisive effect on his behavior unconsciously. There are also elements of the unconscious which are shared by everyone. Jung studied ancient symbols and myths, and analyzed the dreams of his contemporaries. He came to the conclusion that many symbols recur even though modern man may not have known of the ancient representations. Such symbols which have universal significance are said by Jung to be part of the "collective unconscious," and are called "archetypes."

Finally, Jung coined the term "anima" to refer to an unconscious feminine aspect within a man through which he can to some extent intuitively comprehend the nature of women. The references in *Demian* to masculine traits in a woman, or feminine traits in a man, are based on this concept, and many apparent **allusions** to homosexuality, which some critics are fond of pointing out, can likewise be explained on the basis of Jung's concept. The several aspects of personality, in Jung's formulation, must be integrated if a person, man or woman, is to attain fulfillment. They must accordingly always be considered as parts of a whole, and not as isolated components.

## HESSE'S POPULARITY

The history of Hesse's popularity in Germany and America is complex and, on the surface at least, enigmatic. He was a competent popular novelist and essayist during the first two decades of this century and enjoyed a certain following among the German reading public at that time. Upon the publication of *Demian* in 1919, he immediately became one of the heroes of one segment of the younger generation in Germany. His disillusionment with the war and his visionary, even mystical attitude toward the future contributed greatly to his popularity and to his success (although it should be noted that some Germans reproached him for his lack of patriotism during the war). His popularity in German-speaking countries remained high until the early 1930s, when Hitler assumed power in Germany. Because they were largely unpolitical, Hesse's books were not immediately burned and banned in Germany, but his work was not encouraged or even approved by the Nazi hierarchy. Many important intellectuals and writers, both German and non-German, praised Hesse highly. Among these are T.S. Elliot, André Gide, and Thomas Mann. After a brief period of popularity in Europe following the Second World War, Hesse's reputation began to decline, both among academicians and the younger generation of readers. At the present time, Hesse's reputation in Germany is at an all-time low. The young radicals, especially, have no use for his writings since they associate them with the Romantic past - including Nazism! - which they desire to overcome and leave behind.

Hesse has been widely translated into non-European languages, and his reception in India and Japan, especially, has been consistently favorable, and not subject to the ups and downs which mark his popularity in Germany and in America. Hesse was proud of the fact that readers in Eastern countries appreciated his works, which contain many elements of Eastern philosophy.

The history of Hesse's reception in America is quite different from that of his reception in Germany. Although several of his works had appeared in translation throughout the years, he was all but unknown in this country when he received the Nobel Prize for Literature in 1946. The American press for the most part ignored him, even when he received this prestigious award. It was only in the late 1950s that Americans began to become interested in his work. Today, of course, he has become a cult figure. Hesse is without doubt one of the very favorite authors of college-age Americans. Similarly, most of the serious scholarly criticism on Hesse in recent years has been written in English, and most of the important books have been written by North Americans.

It is certainly easy to see why American youth is interested in Hesse. The problems with which he deals in his stories and novels have meaning for young people in this country today. His treatment of adolescence, the problems of growing up, authority, rebellion, the "establishment," sex, human relationships, and, to a lesser extent, drugs, is significant and "relevant." Likewise, many young people share Hesse's interest in Oriental philosophy and in a non-dogmatic theology. It must, however, be pointed out that many important elements of Hesse's thought are overlooked by the majority of his admirers. For example, one often sees a devotion to self-discipline and hard work directed toward the achievement of some specific goal in Hesse's work. Especially Demian, Siddhartha, and Joseph Knecht attain a remarkable amount of self-discipline while still quite young, and it becomes clear in the respective works that the success and happiness of these characters is possible only because of their earlier rigorous training. If Hesse does not share the Protestant ethic of hard work, he nonetheless sees and portrays in his novels the necessity of building one's life on a firm foundation. Many of his works also show the other side of the coin - the results of not building one's life on a firm foundation (e.g., Klein and Knulp, who is much less happy than the more disciplined wanderer Goldmund). Hesse in no way respects bourgeois narrow-mindedness, complacency, and resistance to change at all cost; but neither does he express approval of destructive rebellion for its own sake. The freedom of Hesse's characters is a reflection of a successful, integrated life; they are slaves neither to tradition nor to their own weaknesses.

It is especially ironic that Hesse has become a folk hero and a model for an entire generation, for Hesse's most important **theme** throughout his mature works is the necessity of each individual finding his own way in life, rather than following the doctrine or teachings of an authority-figure, however noble or admirable such a figure may be. Often the incidentals of Hesse's novels and stories-rebellion against authority, sexual freedom, etc. - are religiously praised and faithfully followed by his young readers, who thereby completely lose touch with the fundamental aspect of Hesse's thought: the value of an individual's determining, choosing, and continually reexamining his own values. Surely nothing is more foreign to Hesse than the idea that "I have found the way, and there is no other." And this is indeed the narrow-minded philosophy of some of those who have chosen Hesse as their hero and mentor.

It is difficult to predict what direction Hesse's future popularity will take. More and more of his works are being translated into English - short stories, essays on various subjects, poems, autobiographical sketches, indeed almost anything will be eagerly purchased by his faithful reading public. Sooner or later a reaction must take place. Much of Hesse's short prose fiction is not especially rich or rewarding; his essays are to a great extent dated and have only historical interest; his range as a poet is narrow and poetry is in any event difficult to translate, or to appreciate in translation; and his autobiographical works are unquestionably among his least successful. It is to be hoped that these minor works will enable the American reader to more fully appreciate the complexity of Hesse, without detracting from his truly great novels and short stories.

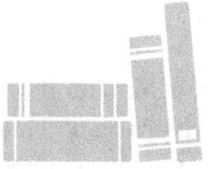

# SIDDHARTHA

## COMPOSITION, PUBLICATION, AND TRANSLATION OF SIDDHARTHA

### GENESIS AND PUBLICATION

*Siddhartha* was begun in 1919, when Hesse was enjoying one of his most happy and productive periods. He quickly finished the first four chapters and published them in a periodical. He turned then to other projects (including the story *Klingsor's Last Summer*), and resumed work on *Siddhartha* later in the winter of 1919-1920. He completed the second portion, consisting of chapters five through eight, and then found himself unable to complete his story.

Hesse recorded his thoughts from these months in a diary which he published in 1932, in the German periodical *Corona*. In this diary, Hesse speaks of many things, especially of his feeling of loneliness and isolation and his inability to work. He is depressed by the many letters which he is receiving from Germans who rebuke him for his lack of patriotism for his native land during the recent war. He calls 1920 the "most unproductive year" of his life, and exclaims "Oh, how I wish I were able to (… work!") *Siddhartha*, specifically, is a problem. As long as he was depicting Siddhartha's seeking, learning, suffering, and errors, he was able to proceed without difficulty. But now that it is time to portray the triumphant Siddhartha, he finds that it is impossible to go on.

In several lengthy and highly interesting passages, Hesse discusses the development of his interest in Indian thought, and his changing ideas on this important subject. Although he has been studying India intensively for some twenty years, only recently has his interest extended beyond philosophy to narrower questions of religion and theology. Buddhism, especially, has attracted his attention and he sees in it a relationship to Christian Protestantism. Hesse also comments on the figure of the Buddha, to some extent echoing Siddhartha's sentiments. Although Buddha undoubtedly did attain Nirvana, Hesse says, modern man cannot follow his path-each man must rather find his own way to his own goal.

In the course of the published "diary" fragment-which is actually a polished, if highly personal, essay-Hesse states that he is overcoming his period of inactivity, and the final words are: "*Siddhartha* is once again present. Things are moving forward." He did soon complete the novel and it was published in its entirety in 1992 under the title *Siddhartha: An Indic Poetic Work*.

## TRANSLATION

An English version by Hilda Rosner appeared in 1951. This translation has been reprinted many times, and was for some years the most popular of Hesse's works in English. Like all of Hesse's novels, it is currently available in this country in paperback. Although not without weaknesses (no translation, it should be pointed out, is ever entirely without weaknesses), this is an entirely satisfactory and faithful rendering of Hesse's novel in both style and content.

## EXPLANATION OF SELECTED EASTERN TERMINOLOGY

Atman: a complicated Sanskrit term which has many meanings: breath, the self, the Universal Self.

Brahma: the Lord of Creation.

Brahman: 1) the Central Power of the universe; 2) (also spelled "Brahmin") a member of the highest of the four Hindu classes. Typically a Brahman, such as Siddhartha's father, is an erudite man who studies and teaches the scriptures and performs religious ceremonies.

Jetavana: historically, a garden, one of the residences of Gotama, the Buddha.

Kama: the Hindu god of desire.

Krishna: one of the most famous incarnations of Vishnu, the Preserver, in Hindu theology.

Lakshmi: the Hindu goddess of beauty and good fortune.

Magadha: an important kingdom in ancient India.

Mara: in Buddhist theology, the spirit of evil and enemy of the Buddha.

Maya: illusion.

Nirvana: in Buddhism, a state, extremely difficult to define (or to attain!) characterized by a release from the bonds of suffering.

Om: defined in the novel as "Perfection" (in the chapter "By the River").

Prajapati: Creator or Supreme Deity.

Sakya: a clan name of Gotama the Buddha.

Samana: a mendicant ascetic.

Sansara: the world characterized by endless repetition, without Nirvana.

Satyam: Truth and Reality.

Upanishads: mystical utterances at the conclusion of the Vedas.

Vedas: ancient scriptural literature of Hinduism.

Vishnu: the Preserver, a major Hindu deity.

## HESSE AND INDIA

India had long fascinated the romantically-inclined Germans. Many of the poets of German Romanticism were interested in India as well as in other Eastern cultures, and Goethe shared this interest. The Indic tradition in German literature remained alive during the nineteenth century, and a number of authors of that period translated or imitated works from Indian literature. Hesse was familiar with much of this long and rich tradition.

Hesse's own family background provided a specific link to India. Both of his parents had lived as missionaries in India and had grown familiar with the culture of that land. His grandfather had likewise been a missionary in India, and was quite knowledgeable in the area of Indian philosophy and theology, as was Hesse's own father. Both men amassed impressive collections of books on the subject. Hermann accordingly had access to the mysteries of India from several sources. Early in his childhood he acquired a keen interest in the East, an interest which he was never to lose.

Shortly after 1900, Hesse began the serious study of Indian culture. His interest deepened, and as the years passed he fabricated an idealized image of this distant land. As his own personal problems grew more acute, he came to think of India as a land of salvation. In 1991 he undertook a voyage to India, seeking peace and happiness. In a sense his voyage was a failure. Hesse was not able to apply India's magic to his own situation and his specific personal problems were not solved. But on a higher level his voyage did prove to be a success. While in India Hesse came to believe in "Oneness," "Harmony," or whatever this mysterious aspect of Indian thought might be called in Western languages which have no adequate terminology for it. Hesse began to search for a means of symbolically expressing this feeling and finally, after much labor and anguish, was able to find this expression in *Siddhartha*.

Hesse's interest in India did not cease with the publication of *Siddhartha*. The East is important in several of the later works, especially, of course, in *Journey to the East*, but also in *The Glass Bead Game*.

## SOURCES OF SIDDHARTHA: THE EAST

*Siddhartha*, set in India, is subtitled an "Indic Poetic Work," and it clearly owes much to Indian religions. But the question of the exact nature of Hesse's debt to various aspects of Indian religion and philosophy in *Siddhartha* is quite complicated and deserves detailed discussion. Elements of both Hindu and Buddhist thought are present and it is useful to make distinctions between them when the sources of the novel are discussed.

## BUDDHISM

"Siddhartha" is one of the names of the historical Gotama, and the life of Hesse's character resembles that of his historical counterpart to some extent. *Siddhartha* is by no means a fictional life of Buddha, but it does contain numerous references to Buddha and his teachings.

The basic teaching of Buddha is formulated in the Four Noble Truths and the Eightfold Path. Proceeding from the premise that suffering exists and that a release from it must be found, Buddha constructed his system. The First Noble Truth is the fact of suffering. The Second Truth is that suffering arises from human desire for something, and that this desire can never be satisfied. The Third Truth is that there is a way to achieve a release from suffering. And the Fourth Truth prescribes the manner of overcoming suffering and attaining true knowledge.

The first two steps in the Eightfold Path, which leads to the cessation of suffering, are right understanding and right resolution; a person must first discover and experience the correctness of the Four Noble Truths (it is not sufficient to profess a superficial belief), and then resolve to follow the correct path. The next three steps likewise form a kind of unit: right speech, right behavior, and right livelihood. These reflect the external aspects of a person's life, which must not be neglected. The interior disciplines constitute the final three steps: right efforts, right mindfulness, and right contemplation. By this means, the follower of Buddha can arrive at Nirvana.

One critic, Leroy R. Shaw, has pointed out that *Siddhartha* is divided into two parts of four and eight chapters, and proceeds from this insight to interpret the work as an illustration of Buddha's Truths and Path; in the first chapter Siddhartha learns the existence of suffering, in the fifth (which corresponds to the first step of the Path) he begins his journey along the correct path, etc. Shaw, then, comes to the conclusion that at the end "the difference between Siddhartha and Gotama, which had seemed so vast to the seeker at his meeting with the sage, becomes non-existent." This is certainly true in one respect; both Gotama and Siddhartha have arrived at a final condition of Harmony (although the nature of the Harmony differs considerably). But Siddhartha's way was clearly not that of Buddha. The division of four and eight seems nevertheless to allude to the Truths and the Path, since a more natural division of the novel, considering its structure, would be into three sections of four chapters each.

Other aspects of Buddha's teachings are also of interest. Buddha was rather logical, scientific, and rational in his approach. He did not speak of supernatural phenomena or an afterlife, and he dismissed the possibility of miracles. Buddha taught self-reliance. He had little use for rituals and formalistic laws, and he urged each man to work out his own salvation-which would, of course, be possible only within the framework of the Four Noble Truths and the Eightfold Path. The historical Gotama, like the figure in *Siddhartha*, taught that love and deep attachment to anyone or anything was wrong, since it leads to suffering. Buddha never defined the state of Nirvana as he understood it, beyond saying that in it the cessation of suffering is attained, and that this is accomplished by the absolute extinction of the will.

## HINDUISM

Elements of this Indian religion are also present in *Siddhartha*. Hinduism is not as dogmatic as Christianity, or even as Buddhism. One important - perhaps the most important - aspect of Hinduism is the concept of the Search or Quest for Truth. Whereas the Buddhist and the Christian each has a specific (if ultimately unknowable) goal and general guidelines which he can follow to attain it, for the Hindu the quest itself is all-important. As T. W. Organ aptly remarks, "The Christian says, 'Seek and ye shall find.' But the Hindu says, 'Seek and ye shall find.'"

There are obvious parallels between Hinduism and *Siddhartha*, and these have not been overlooked by critics. Most critics even assert that Hinduism is a more significant source for the book than is Buddhism. Eugene F. Timpe, for example, in a study which is methodologically similar to that of Shaw, has analyzed parallels between *Siddhartha* and the Bhagavad Gita, an important poetical document of the Hindu religion. Timpe maintains "that Hesse was influenced largely by the Bhagavad Gita when he wrote his book and that the **protagonist** was groping his way along the path prescribed by the Bhagavad Gita." Hesse was indeed familiar with this important work, and a comparison between it and *Siddhartha* is rewarding.

As Timpe points out, the basic central problems of *Siddhartha* and the Gita are similar: how can the hero attain a state of total happiness and serenity by means of a long and arduous path?

The development of each character is divided into three distinct stages: in *Siddhartha* there are - as one would expect in Hesse - innocence, followed by knowledge ("sin"), which, together, lead to a higher state of innocence accompanied by increased awareness and consciousness.

In the Gita the path is similar, but not identical. It goes from action to knowledge to wisdom. Action is the first stage in the hero's long road to perfection. Not arbitrary human actions are meant, but rather a form of action produced by acceptance of the Divine element in an individual. The person then moves toward knowledge-knowledge of the Self and of the Absolute, which ultimately are revealed to be identical. The renouncing of all earthly attachments is a necessary component of each of the first two stages of development. A kind of self-fulfillment is stressed. An individual must find and follow his own path, for the ultimate goal cannot be attained by any form of imitation, however noble and admirable the model or teacher may be. The final, and highest, stage is characterized by reverence and wisdom. The seeker reveres and even worships the Absolute, with which he is identical.

Direct parallels with *Siddhartha* can be drawn. Hesse's hero seeks his own path to fulfillment. Although his path is one of trial and error, he is always at least unconsciously aware of the nature of his quest. He comes to realize that seeking a goal will ultimately prove to be limiting. From Vasudeva he acquires knowledge of what true action is. Finally, he is transfigured and attains wisdom.

## HESSE'S COMMENTS ON INDIAN RELIGION

In 1932 Hess published a "diary fragment" written some twelve years earlier, during the composition of *Siddhartha*. In this interesting and revealing essay, he comments extensively on Indian religion. His remarks are important, but should not be accepted uncritically as the "final word" on any of the subjects which he discusses.

In the diary Hesse acknowledges his long-standing interest in India. He says that this interest was previously largely confined to questions of philosophy, but that recently has become more oriented toward religion. He sees Buddhism as a kind of "Reformation," but - like all religious reformations - it eventually tends to be more destructive than constructive. (Ultimately Buddhism denies rather than affirms life.) Hesse discusses the Buddhistic conception of Nirvana, and observes that whereas he previously accepted the doctrine, he now inclines toward the belief that God respects individuality. Buddha may well have reached Nirvana, but other men will not be able to find a "shortcut" by following and imitating him. Hesse rejects the rationalism of Buddha's teachings which, he says, previously attracted him. The mystical aspects of Christianity acquire correspondingly more appeal. Hesse, then, feels that he is moving away from the philosophical position of Buddhism.

Many of the **themes** of *Siddhartha* can be seen reflected in Hesse's discussion of Buddhism in the essay. The title character of Hesse's story objects to the negative (destructive) aspects of Gotama's teaching. He rejects Gotama's way as a model for himself, although he recognizes the greatness of the Buddha and he insists upon the right to reject all teachers in favor of his own individual path to fulfillment.

## AUTOBIOGRAPHICAL ASPECTS

As the essay discussed immediately above indicates, Siddhartha's philosophical views correspond closely to Hesse's.

The simplicity of the plot enables the ideas to emerge clearly and distinctly, and an unusually close correspondence between Hesse and his fictional character emerges. In addition, there is an important individual parallel between Siddhartha and Hesse. Hesse's own rejection of the life chosen for him by his father closely resembles Siddhartha's refusal to follow in the footsteps of his father, the Brahman, and imitate his life.

## WESTERN, "FAUSTIAN" ELEMENTS

Siddhartha is by no means an entirely "Eastern" figure. As critics have pointed out, he also has strong elements of the independent "Faustian" spirit, which is typical on Western man. Siddhartha, like Faust, strives desperately and unrelentingly for knowledge. Siddhartha does not wish to transcend, but to conquer life. In this respect he to some extent stands in contrast to Govinda, who represents the passive Oriental attitude toward life and its suffering.

## CHRISTIANITY

Two major connections with Christianity are present in *Siddhartha*. In a short essay from the year 1930, Hesse succinctly formulates his conception of the important problems of the work: "My Siddhartha glorifies love, and not some form of intellectual awareness. This, together with the book's rejection of dogma and central concern with the experience of unity, could be taken as a return to Christianity and even as a genuinely Protestant characteristic."

The first Christian trait is the importance of love. Siddhartha, like Jesus and unlike Buddha, affirms love and perfects this virtue within himself. Siddhartha's serenity, with its central component of love, resembles that of the very early Christians (as portrayed, for example, in such popularized works as *The Robe* and *Ben Hur*), rather than that of the typical Eastern sage who has attained Nirvana and has removed himself from such "earthly" attachments as love.

The second aspect of Siddhartha's Christianity is its Protestant character. Hesse's assessment, given in the quote above, is remarkably perceptive, and it is even possible to draw fairly close parallels between Siddhartha and Martin Luther, the leading figure of the Protestant Reformation. Basically, Luther objected to the right of the Catholic Church to dictate the path of each individual to heaven. He insisted that every person must find his own way (to be sure, with the guidance of the Holy Scriptures). For the Protestant, faith alone leads to salvation; good works will presumably naturally follow from faith, and hence are not of primary concern. Siddhartha, too, does not worry about his specific actions, as long as he feels as though he is basically on the right path. Luther once said in a letter, "Be a sinner and sin strongly, but more strongly have faith and rejoice in Christ." Siddhartha, too, "sins strongly" while striving for his goal, in which he rejoices more strongly. For Siddhartha, the forms and rituals of the Brahman priests are insignificant, just as for Luther the forms of the Roman Catholic Church seemed empty. Siddhartha's "faith," of course, is not Christian; he believes in Atman, in the unity of all things - and in his own power to attain this unity. Even Luther's firmness of conviction is reminiscent of Siddhartha. Luther's famous words "Here I stand. I can do no other" could serve as a motto for Siddhartha's life.

Hesse expressed similar thoughts on the subject of religion, specifically Protestant Christianity, in a "Short Autobiographical Note" from the year 1925. In this note he says that a true

Protestant is just as much on guard against his own church as against any other. Siddhartha is a "protestant" insofar as he first rejects the "other" church - the religious traditions and institutions of his father. He later rejects the Buddha's teachings too. But most significantly, he is continually testing his own beliefs and values, lest his way of life become formalized (as it in fact does at the end of his middle period).

## THEMES

The primary **theme** of *Siddhartha* is the individual's difficult search for self-fulfillment. Both the means used by the hero in his quest and the nature of the fulfillment which he finally attains are important.

## TEACHERS

Siddhartha and Govinda use different approaches in their search for truth and harmony. Early in life, Govinda listens to the Buddha and is convinced of the validity of his teachings. He completely follows his teacher in every respect, completely devoting his life to the pursuit of these ideals. Govinda leads a happy, peaceful life, but he feels that he has not attained the level of understanding and serenity enjoyed by his great teacher. Near the end of his life he once again seeks the advice of a teacher who has apparently found the secret for which he is searching. In this instance the teacher is Siddhartha, and from Siddhartha's smile-not from his words!-Govinda finally gains at least some (emotional) insight into the nature of Unity.

Siddhartha likewise listens with great respect to the words of the Buddha. He does not become a disciple, but he nonetheless learns three important things as a result of this encounter: 1) it is possible to achieve one's goal in life, for the Buddha has done so; 2) the general nature of the goal, for himself, must be self-fulfillment; and 3) this goal can be achieved only through his own effort, and not by following a teacher. As in *Demian*, Nietzsche's influence is apparent here; the reader is strongly reminded of Nietzsche's Zarathustra, who exhorts his listeners not to follow him, but rather to excel him, to go beyond his stage of development. The Hindu notion of the importance of the quest itself, vis-a-vis the specific goal, is also reflected.

## NATURE OF THE GOAL

Siddhartha's final sense of fulfillment is mystical and hence cannot be defined with precision. In this respect, it resembles the Nirvana of Buddhism, which also cannot be defined exactly. In general, Siddhartha's final serenity is based on the realization that all things are one. Even an apparently insignificant object such as a stone shares a common existence with the most noble aspects of creation. Death is not to be viewed as the end of life, but as the release of the person into eternity-into the eternity of the universe, to be sure, and not into the eternity of a religious afterlife. The most important aspect of Siddhartha's final state of awareness is love, an unselfish, undirected love. As he tells Govinda, the world should be (intuitively) loved rather than (rationally) studied and explained.

## GENERATION GAP

An important aspect of the **theme** is the relationship between father and son. When Siddhartha is approximately twenty years old, or slightly younger, he leaves his father, never to return. The father, a happy, successful, and thoroughly admirable man, cannot understand why Siddhartha does not wish to follow in his footsteps. To his credit, however, the father soon comes to see that Siddhartha must be allowed to find his own mode of life and establish his own values. Reluctantly, he allows his son to depart with his blessings.

The situation recurs when Siddhartha's own son rejects the life chosen for him by his father. Siddhartha, as Vasudeva points out, has not learned from his own experience. Just as Siddhartha demanded the right to reject the admirable life of his father, so too does Siddhartha's son. Siddhartha, like his own father secure in the knowledge that he has found the "truth," for a long time fails to recognize that he was able to gain access to this truth only by means of long years of seeking and suffering, by trial and error. He cannot understand why his son must leave without learning from his example, and without profiting from his long years of experience. Here he forgets an important principle which he formulated years earlier. When he spoke to the Buddha he said that he could not judge for anyone else, and that he had to judge for himself. Now he violates both parts of this earlier principle.

## FATHER-WORLD AND MOTHER-WORLD

The division of the world into two poles is a common **theme** in Hesse's writings. These two poles are usually represented as the Father-World (intellect, reason, spirit, stability or permanence, discipline), and the Mother-World (emotion, love, fertility, birth, death, transience, nature, the senses). While this symbolism is of greater importance in other works, such as *Demian* and *The Glass Bead Game*, it is also present and is consistently developed in *Siddhartha*. For example, Siddhartha's father admires his son's intelligence and thirst for knowledge, and he wants him to become a priest and a man of learning; his mother, on the other hand, admires his physical appearance and his natural grace.

Govinda is a representative of the Father-World. Early in life he most admires Siddhartha on account of his intellect, and at the end of his life he feels uneasy when Siddhartha requests that he kiss him on the forehead (a display of emotion). The Buddha, too, is of this world. It is explicitly stated in the novel that he has "brought the cycle of rebirth to a halt" - thereby excluding the most fundamental aspect of the Mother-World.

Siddhartha's position vis-a-vis the two worlds changes during the course of the novel. Early in life he unites the virtues of each of the poles (as is reflected, for example, in the different qualities admired by his father and his mother.) When he joins the Samanas he rejects entirely the World of the Mother, as the narrator indicates when he reports that Siddhartha felt scorn when he saw such things as funerals and death, lovers, mothers and their children, and priests making decisions relating to the proper time for the sowing of crops (all aspects of the World of the Mother). Later, Siddhartha comes to accept the Mother as part of the Unity of all things and thereby is able to attain his final state of serenity. There is a similarity between the final stage of Siddhartha and that of Goldmund in *Narcissus and Goldmund*. Just as Siddhartha, who accepts the World of the Mother, is shown to be in a way superior to Govinda, who is limited to the World of the Father, so is Goldmund in a way superior to the more limited, if admirable, Narcissus.

## IMPORTANT SYMBOLS

### The River

In *Siddhartha*, this one symbol far surpasses all others in importance. Suggesting fluidity as well as the paradoxical union of permanence and flux (it seems to remain always constant, although the individual drops of water of which it is composed are constantly changing), the river is an age-old symbol suggesting eternity and a kind of spiritual understanding or communion. Leonard Cohen's song "Suzanne" is a recent example of the symbolic use of the river which is in some respects similar to that found in *Siddhartha*.

The river, as a body of water, also suggests the world of the Mother, the world of nature. Water is the source of life and is necessary to maintain life; it is associated with fertility. Water frequently appears in literature with this symbolic value. The significance of the natural world of fertility, creation, love, and death, as opposed to the artificial unchanging world of the intellect (the Father-World) is more fully developed in other works of Hesse, especially in *Narcissus and Goldmund* and *The Glass Bead Game*. But Siddhartha rejects the Father-World of the Samanas in favor of the world of the senses, and eventually he attains a synthesis of the two.

A river is mentioned in the important first paragraph of the story, where we are told that Siddhartha grew up on a river bank. Siddhartha was, then, exposed to the river during his childhood, which symbolically suggests that he was receptive to the "message" of the river - the Unity of all things.

The river is conspicuously absent in the description of Siddhartha's time among the Samanas, for their world is sterile and their way of life does not lead to unity. When he tells Govinda why he feels that he must leave then, he repeatedly says that he is "thirsty," reflecting his unconscious knowledge of the importance of water, and of the Mother-World which it represents. When Siddhartha leaves the Samanas, the narrator comments that he becomes aware of the beauties of nature, especially of the river.

The river which Siddhartha crosses at this stage of his life retains the symbolic values discussed above, and also adds a new one: it is a boundary between the world of the Samanas and the world of the senses, between the two worlds which Siddhartha must learn to synthesize.

It is casually mentioned that a river flows through the town in which Kamala lives and in which Siddhartha dwells for some twenty years. This suggests on the one hand that the world portrayed here is basically the World of the Mother, of nature; but the symbolism is not developed and accordingly Siddhartha's gradual loss of a feeling of self-esteem can be related to his lack of contact with the river during these years.

Siddhartha's rejuvenation begins when he leaves Kamala and his worldly life, and comes upon the very river which he crossed some twenty years previously. At his low ebb, Siddhartha experiences despair and desires death. But these thoughts disappear when he stares into the water and hears the mystical sound "Om," "Perfection." While he sleeps, the soft sound of the water has a soothing effect and when he awakens he feels greatly refreshed.

Siddhartha rapidly comes to depend upon the river. He learns from it the secret of the Unity of all things, and he is soothed by its soft voice. As Vasudeva points out, the river knows everything, and people who are receptive can learn from it. For most people, he adds, the river is an obstacle - as it is for the many weary travelers who must cross it. But for a select few it is not an obstacle, but rather something profound, something sacred. Siddhartha grows in wisdom and he attempts to formulate his understanding of what the river has taught him: there is no past or future, everything is present - there is a mystical unity in all things.

The river is instrumental in enabling Siddhartha to overcome his final obstacle, the lingering sorrow and pain he feels because of his son's departure. One day when Siddhartha sets out to search for his son, the river speaks to him - but not in its usual soothing tone. This time the river laughs at him. Siddhartha looks into the water and sees his own reflection, which reminds him, however, of his father. He is reminded of the pain he caused his own father years earlier when he departed, never to return, and gradually perceives that the river is pointing out to him the repetitious nature of events. Nothing is new, everything is an integral part of a unified whole, including such things as the inevitable separation of fathers and sons. The various voices of the river, the laughter and the sorrow, seem to merge, and finally Siddhartha hears only the sum: the word "Om."

## The Smile

A second important symbol in *Siddhartha* is the smile. Each of the three characters in the story who attain a final state of complete serenity is characterized by a beautiful smile which reflects their peaceful, harmonious state. In each case this smile is a completely natural phenomenon; it cannot be created at will by people who have not attained the prerequisite state of harmony with life.

The first character who is described as possessing this smile is Gotama, the Buddha. When Siddhartha first sees him, he recognizes him immediately, largely on account of this mysterious smile. Gotama is imperturbable and he retains his smile - and his equanimity - even when Siddhartha engages in debate with him. As Gotama turns to leave, it is his smile which most deeply impresses Siddhartha, for in it the peace and saintliness of the Buddha is epitomized. The narrator comments that Siddhartha was to remember this smile for the rest of his life.

Vasudeva also possesses the mystical smile of peace and harmony. A man of very few words, the ferryman often allows his smile to speak for him, and it is a more effective agent of expression than any words could possibly have been. Like the Buddha, Vasudeva is satisfied that he is at peace with the world, and with existence.

Siddhartha does not possess this radiant smile at first. He sees it in Gotama and Vasudeva and recognizes its significance, but is too engrossed in physical things to be able to smile serenely himself. First, with the Samanas, he concentrates on mastering his bodily needs. Then, through Kamala and Kamaswami, he learns to enjoy sensual pleasures and soon masters this aspect of life. Finally his love of his son and then his sense of pain over losing the boy keep him from attaining serenity. Only when the ferryman takes his final leave, and Siddhartha gazes into his face and listens to the message of the river, does he finally acquire a radiant smile like that of his friend, signifying his own attainment of a state of Unity.

The smile, like the river, suggests perfection and unity, and it is Siddhartha's smile that makes such a strong impression on Govinda at the close of the story. Just as Siddhartha perceived unity and perfection by listening to and gazing into the river, Govinda comes to feel at least an intimation of the Unity of all things by looking into Siddhartha's face and experiencing a genuine emotional response to the saintless revealed in his smile.

The smile and one aspect of the much more complicated river are closely related. Each suggests unity and harmony, and each is associated with Siddhartha at key junctures in his life. Although Gotama possesses the smile, the absence of the river as a significant factor in his life suggests that the smile is symbolic of one aspect of existence, whereas the river must also signify the World of the Mother, a world with which the Buddha has no contact.

## Structure

Externally, the book is divided into two distinct parts. The first part, which comprises four chapters, describes Siddhartha's childhood and adolescent years, and reaches its conclusion when he leaves Govinda and the Buddha to seek a new life in the world of nature, renouncing his past life of asceticism. The first part, then, is devoted to his years of preparation for life, and the second part-which includes the remaining eight chapters of the book-to his years of experiencing life, and his eventual attainment of a sense of serenity and harmony with life. As was pointed out above, the division of four and eight may suggest the Four Noble Truths and the Eightfold Path of Buddha.

According to a different structural principle, the work is seen to be divided into three more or less equal sections of four chapters each. The first four describe Siddhartha's years of preparation for life; the second group of four is devoted to his experiences in mastering the arts of love (with Kamala) and business (with Kamaswami); and the final group portrays his later years, when he lives near the river and comes to understand its message. Although it is impossible to determine exactly the amount of time which passes in the novel, we are told that Siddhartha is a young man when he meets Kamala, and that he is in his forties when he leaves her. He spends many years by the river, and so it would seem that each of the three groups of four chapters describes a period of approximately twenty years, or about one-third of Siddhartha's life.

It is significant that the novel has two structural principles, one external and one internal. Each division is appropriate; it is natural to divide Siddhartha's life according to either one. The presence of two different but equally valid structural principles corroborates one of the novel's main themes: the necessity of avoiding superficial generalizations and oversimplifications, and of finding harmony by means of the successful integration and synthesis of disparate elements.

## Style

The style of the novel is extremely simple, in keeping with its plot, **theme**, and general tone. The **syntax** is uncomplicated and with the exception of a few technical terms from Indian philosophy, the vocabulary is straightforward and rather limited. Frequent use is made of leitmotifs, parallelism, and repetition, and-in the original German, at least - the language is rhythmical and lyrical. The style is reminiscent of a poetical religious text, and as a critic has pointed out, it has a "meditative" quality; phrases and even words invite the reader to pause for meditation.

## Point of View

The story is told by an omniscient third-person narrator, with frequent direct and indirect quotations of the words and thoughts of various characters, especially of Siddhartha. Almost invariably the narrator looks at things from Siddhartha's perspective, and even when other characters are discussed or quoted, it is always done to throw light on Siddhartha. Even though there is an omniscient narrator, the reader is really being exposed continually to Siddhartha's point of view. A significant break in this pattern can be seen at the very end of the book. When Govinda gazes into Siddhartha's face and responds to what he sees, the narrator's point of view shifts and it is now from Govinda's perspective that we perceive the reality of the world and of the novel.

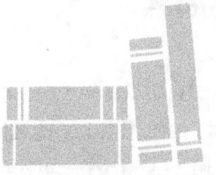

# SIDDHARTHA

## TEXTUAL ANALYSIS

### CHAPTER ONE: THE SON OF THE BRAHMAN

..........................................................................

#### TITLE

At the very beginning, some of the important **themes** of the novel are suggested. Siddhartha is first introduced as his father's son, and the father-son relationship later proves to be of considerable significance. It is also important that the father is a Brahman who rigidly follows this form of life.

#### THEMES AND MOTIFS

All of the important **themes** and motifs of the story are introduced and to some extent developed in the first chapter. The narrator describes Siddhartha's desire to attain unity, and reports Siddhartha's own thoughts on this subject at some length. Forms and rituals, common to his father's religion and way of life, are not enough for Siddhartha; he feels that he must find his own explanation of the world, and he will seek it in "Atman," the innermost self. The sub-theme of the generation gap is also introduced here. Siddhartha holds it to be perfectly natural for him to break away from the way of his father, even though his father is an admirable man who by no means leads a bad life.

## CHARACTERIZATION

The fundamental difference between Siddhartha and Govinda is immediately made clear: Govinda is a follower, while Siddhartha is a leader. Siddhartha has been a good, even a model student and has learned much. But now he feels that he has exhausted the possibilities of his home environment and must move on if he is to be true to himself. He remains courteous and respectful to his father, yet absolutely insists upon his right to lead an independent life of his own choosing.

Govinda comes from a similar background, but he lacks his friend's independent spirit. He senses that the rigid, structured life of the Brahman system is not for him, but he has no conception of what he wants to replace it with. He has ultimate confidence in Siddhartha and is certain that if he follows his friend, he will be led to a higher state of perfection.

## UNITY

The **theme** of Unity is introduced by means of the river symbol and by the mystical word "Om," as well as by the direct commentary of the narrator and of Siddhartha. The frequent **allusion** to the river parallels Siddhartha's constant thoughts about unity and his incipient plans to strive for it. He already has learned the meaning of the word "Om," and is able to enter a deep trance through repeating it and contemplating its deep significance. Govinda here, as always, has made less progress than has his friend. He has studied, but not thoroughly mastered, the art of meditation. The reader sees that Govinda will always remain a step behind Siddhartha in whatever he undertakes.

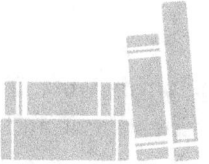

# SIDDHARTHA

## TEXTUAL ANALYSIS

### CHAPTER TWO: WITH THE SAMANAS

**TITLE**

Whereas Siddhartha previously was associated with the life of his father, a Brahman, he is now a Samana. In a way this marks a forward step for Siddhartha. This is not so much because the life of a Samana is intrinsically better than that of a Brahman, but more because Siddhartha has independently chosen this new way of life, whereas he had merely accepted his previous mode of existence. But Siddhartha is still only one member of a group, even though the nature of the group has changed. He is categorized as one of the Samanas and is hence still far from his desired state of individual self-realization.

**APPRENTICESHIP**

Siddhartha's time of learning continues. From his erudite father he learned how to read and write, and from the Samanas he perfects the ability to wait (to be patient) and to fast. He continually exercises and improves his intellect-his ability to think - and accordingly develops the fifth and last of the skills which serve him so well during his years with Kamala and Kamaswami. Siddhartha expresses the sentiment that too much formal study and the acquisition of too much formal knowledge can hamper a person in his search for Atman. He sees that the old Samanas have not attained it, even though their life may be preferable to that of a Brahman, so he decides that he must depart. When Siddhartha masters the old Samana as he takes his leave, he demonstrates that he has indeed derived the maximum possible benefit from this stage of his life.

## THE GOAL

At this stage of Siddhartha's life, as he joins the Samanas, he strives single-mindedly for a specific goal: to empty himself of all human emotions and let his Self die, so that he might awaken in the state of perfection. Gradually he comes to see the error of this way of life. This set of rules, this doctrine-just like that of his father-is incomplete and must be rejected. It is no more correct, for Siddhartha, to be one Samana (of many) than to be one Brahman (of many).

It may seem inappropriate to speak of Siddhartha's "goal," since one of the major **themes** of the book is the danger of having an unchanging long range goal. Siddhartha has an indefinite long range goal, but he does not define or limit it, as does, for example, the Buddha. He has several specific goals during the course of the story, but this in no way detracts from the open nature of his ultimate goal. The attainment of specific goals, in fact, is a necessary part of his progression toward his ultimate state of Unity.

## CHARACTERIZATION

Siddhartha's independence is further stressed in this chapter. He quickly sees that he was wrong in assuming that he could find his own answer "with the Samanas." He here displays elements of the Western, Faustian man by saying that he has sought truth and come to the conclusion that it is not possible for man to know anything. As before, Govinda's actions and attitude show him to be more traditional. He hesitates to follow Siddhartha in his more radical conclusions, and feels torn between his loyalty to his friend, whom he still greatly admires, and to traditional institutions, for which he also has considerable respect.

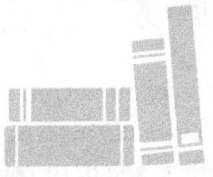

# SIDDHARTHA

## TEXTUAL ANALYSIS

## CHAPTER THREE: GOTAMA

### TITLE

This is the first of three chapters which are named after individual persons and the name suggests the importance of Gotama, the Buddha, for the development of the lives of Siddhartha and Govinda.

### THE DEBATE

The lengthy exchange of words between Siddhartha and Gotama is one of the most important parts of the entire novel. First Siddhartha points out a philosophical inconsistency in Gotama's teachings: if the world is perfectly unified and in perfect harmony, why must one "rise above" it? Gotama does not deny the validity of Siddhartha's objection, but rather mildly chides him for his Faustian thirst for knowledge. The objection he (paradoxically) implies, may be valid, but it is immaterial and irrelevant. Gotama offers freedom from suffering, not knowledge and understanding, which lead toward, rather than away from, suffering. Gotama, in effect, seeks to reverse the consequences of Adam's having eaten from the Tree of Knowledge, and restore the world to its former state of harmony-or, as Siddhartha might say, at least create the semblance of such universal harmony. Siddhartha then raises a more serious objection. Gotama, he points out, has truly achieved an elevated state of sanctity and genuine harmony. But it is his way, and only his way; how could anyone else equal or emulate it? His disciples admire him and follow him in all respects; their lives are admirable and worth-while, and they feel that they are on the right path. But they must all fall short of their goal. The path which they are following is not their own, but rather that of Gotama, and what he has attained through experience and reflection can never be reached through mere imitation, however noble the goal or sincere the attempt.

## CHARACTERIZATION

The development of the first two chapters culminates in the third. Siddhartha has studied and rejected Gotama, the ultimate teacher, thereby irrevocably choosing the path of individual experience in his pursuit of self-realization. Govinda, on the other hand, gladly accepts the teachings of the Buddha. Lacking the qualities of Siddhartha which enable his friend to blaze his own trails, Govinda must select a leader and rigidly follow his teachings. He recognizes the superiority of Gotama's to the other systems, and accordingly makes the best choice for him. It would be as foolish and self-destructive for Govinda to attempt to be independent as it would be for Siddhartha to become a passive and docile follower.

In *Siddhartha*, as in most of Hesse's works, the individual is praised for "doing his own thing." But not all people are able to be original trail blazers. If becoming a good follower is "one's thing," then one should choose a model and follow it. Followers, like leaders and outsiders, must continually retain an open mind. Everyone must both continually question his own way of life and respect the right of each of his fellow men to choose his own way of life.

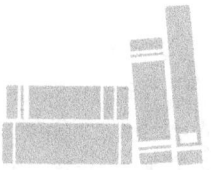

# SIDDHARTHA

## TEXTUAL ANALYSIS

## CHAPTER FOUR: AWAKENING

### TITLE

The transition from innocence to knowledge is suggested. Siddhartha has, of course, in many respects been "awake" throughout his life. But he ignored the sensual side of life, and only now becomes fully aware of it. Furthermore, he now awakens to a fully conscious realization that he must seek knowledge—knowledge of himself and of the world.

### TEACHERS

Siddhartha resolves to reject teachers and doctrines in the future. He indicates, however, that he has carefully considered this decision and has valid reasons for making it. He has, after all, heard the greatest and wisest teacher, and found him lacking. Even listening to the Buddha did not provide him with a sense of fulfillment. But the meeting with Gotama was not entirely without value. Siddhartha sees that his debate served as a sounding board for his own ideas, and that as a result he now has a much better understanding of his own aspirations.

## LONELINESS AND DESPAIR

The role of loneliness in the development of an individual is an important **theme** in all of Hesse's major works. Emil Sinclair, Harry Haller, Goldmund, H.H., and even Joseph Knecht at one time or another go through a period of loneliness which serves to strengthen them. In this chapter, Siddhartha for the first time experiences this sensation. He realizes that he has rejected his previous life, and that he has no new role into which he can easily step. He realizes that he belongs to no class or group of people, and feeling of despair overtakes him. But out of this despair there arises a new hope, a new conviction, a new sense of purpose and identity. It severs the final links with his past- with his father and the Father-World - and he is able to go forward with confidence to discover the World of the Mother.

## STRUCTURE

This chapter marks the end of the first of the two formal structural segments as well as the end of the first of the three periods in Siddhartha's life. The finality of the break in his life is emphasized by the language of the final paragraphs of the chapter, and corresponds to the pause in the action indicated by the break in the external structure.

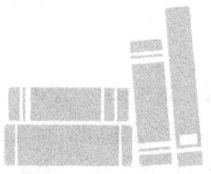

# SIDDHARTHA

## TEXTUAL ANALYSIS

### CHAPTER FIVE: KAMALA

---

#### TITLE

Kamala is the second person in the novel whose personal name serves as a chapter title. This suggests both her significance as an individual being, and her importance in Siddhartha's life.

#### APPRENTICESHIP

Having successfully completed one apprenticeship, Siddhartha joyfully begins a second. He "learns new things" on every step of his journey after leaving Gotama. What he now must learn is nature, the world of everyday life, the World of the Mother. He realizes that experience is necessary to attain wisdom. His previous way of life was quite limited, so he must catch up on what he has missed. He begins to learn about business from Kamaswami and, most important, he is initiated into the art of love by Kamala, the perfect master of the secrets of physical love.

## THE WORLD OF THE MOTHER

As he begins his journey, Siddhartha reflects that he had been right in respecting the intellect (the World of the Father), but now realizes that the senses (the World of the Mother) are also good and noble, and that both worlds must be combined if the Self is to be integrated and attain perfection. He now beholds with wonder and admiration many things for which he previously expressed contempt: mating animals, the cycles of the moon, lush vegetation, beautiful women. Siddhartha does not totally reject the intellect and the Father-World; he continues to practice the discipline which he has learned so well.

Siddhartha is less "psychological" than many of Hesse's works, and the two important dreams are among the comparatively few links between the work and modern psychology. The transformation of Govinda into a woman suggests Siddhartha's turning from asceticism to sensuality and also foreshadows his eventual attainment of unity in which the Father-World and the Mother-World are equal partners.

## SIDDHARTHA'S VOICE

Siddhartha realizes that there is a "voice" within him which he must obey. There is no pattern to the commands given by the voice, and Siddhartha does not attempt to analyze it. But he has confidence in it and, at least at this stage, follows it at all times. This voice represents Siddhartha's newfound sense of values which he himself has formulated. Although he has not articulated and defined his goal, he feels that he now has direction. His voice guides him, reflecting his unconscious awareness of his ultimate goal.

## SIDDHARTHA'S SUPERIORITY AND CONFIDENCE

Perhaps the key to Siddhartha's success is his awareness of his own superior qualities and his confidence in his ability to attain any goal. Siddhartha is an extraordinary person and only the best is good enough for him. At first he is prepared to accept the World of the Mother totally and uncritically. When a beautiful woman attempts to seduce him his immediate inclination - apparently consistent with his new goal of experiencing the world of the senses - is to respond to her advances. But his voice says "no" - not because sensuality is wrong for Siddhartha at this stage of his life, but because the woman, though beautiful, is not worthy of him. Siddhartha can never be satisfied with anything but the very best and since he has not yet become aware of this on a conscious level, his voice must intervene. When he sees Kamala he immediately knows that she is the one for him, and he sets out to win her.

Similarly, he seeks out the best teacher in the business world, Kamaswami. From the start Siddhartha knows that he must never accept a position of subordination vis-a-vis Kamala or Kamaswami. He is in a sense their subordinate, since he lacks skills which they possess and which they can teach him. But he is their equal or superior in other individual respects, and as a human being. Hence he must retain his dignity and equality. His formula for success resembles that of Max Demian: with ability, confidence, and discipline, a person makes his own breaks in life and is in every respect the master of his fate.

# SIDDHARTHA

## TEXTUAL ANALYSIS

### CHAPTER SIX: WITH THE CHILD-PEOPLE

**TITLE**

First it should be noted that Hilda Rosner's translation omits the significant word "child" in the title. An immediate parallel is suggested between this, the second chapter of the second part, and the second chapter of the first part of the novel, "With the Samanas." The reader guesses - and his suspicions are later confirmed - that the parallel will be further developed. The life of the child-people, like that of the Samanas is not evil, but it is not right for Siddhartha. Furthermore, Siddhartha once again faces the danger of becoming merely one member of a group.

The term "child-people" refers to the "ordinary" people, and in fact Rosner uses this term to render Hesse's words in the text of her translation, as, for example, in the last sentence of this chapter. At this time Siddhartha feels that a gulf exists between himself and the ordinary people, the "child people." They are essentially petty and have petty interests, whereas he has long since ceased to share their concerns. Specifically, they are able to experience love, which neither Kamala nor Siddhartha has ever been able to do.

## CHARACTERIZATION

Kamala is skillfully characterized in this chapter. The first impression of her gained in the previous chapter is confirmed. She is a person of substance who has principles which she will not compromise. Siddhartha realizes that she is a unique individual, like himself, and unlike all of those who surround them. He sees that she is more like himself than anyone he has ever known, and he is hence able to "become one" with her.

Siddhartha's characterization is very subtly developed here. He continues his apprenticeship, learning business skills from Kamaswami and the art of love from Kamala - at least during the first part of this period. He seems to retain his independence and superiority. But he feels vaguely uneasy, and his voice "complains" to him. The nature of the complaint is not stated, but it can be deducted. Siddhartha realizes that his business dealings are but a game, a concession on his part to the demands of an external system. In Hesse this is not necessarily evil; Hesse recognizes the occasional need to compromise, so long as truly fundamental principles are not violated. Max Demian, for example, faithfully attends confirmation classes, although he does not believe in Christianity. He does not complain or rebel, since the cause is insignificant, but he rather makes the most of this new experience. So Siddhartha, too, could pursue his business activities as long as they did not interfere with more important things. But Siddhartha has lost sight of his goal and does not understand his voice any longer. His sojourn among the child-people is meaningful only so long as he progresses in some way. He has now learned all he can from Kamala and Kamaswami, and his life begins to be repetitious, as it was with the Samanas after he had mastered their lessons. What he could be learning from these ordinary people, but for some reason does not, is the nature and value of love, a necessary component in his final state of Unity.

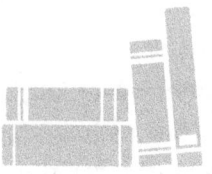

# SIDDHARTHA

## TEXTUAL ANALYSIS

### CHAPTER SEVEN: SANSARA

**TITLE**

Sansara, or "Samsara" as it is usually spelled, is a Buddhist term for the (normal) world, characterized by endless mechanical and meaningless repetition, and without Nirvana. Siddhartha sees that he is caught in this world and wonders why he left the Buddha-whose teaching is based on the assumption that Samsara exists and must be overcome. Siddhartha sees that Samsara is a game and that it can be played a certain number of times with profit, but not indefinitely.

**IMAGERY OF MOTION**

Siddhartha has ceased to make progress, and has become entangled in a seemingly endless and meaningless circular chain of events. In this chapter, **allusion** is frequently made to his condition by means of **imagery** suggesting circular motion and a static state. First, Siddhartha is compared to a potter's wheel which slowly revolves and finally comes to a halt. Inertia creeps into him. He is involved in a "senseless cycle" of acquiring and squandering wealth. In his dream, the songbird lies "stiff" on the bottom of the cage. Siddhartha realizes that he has completely lost contact with his goal, which was formerly not circular but "Onwards, onwards." He, then, first abandons his forward progress in favor of the circular motion of Samsara. And now this circular motion has ground to a halt and he has nothing.

## ATTACHMENT

A significant aspect of Siddhartha's spiritual and physical decline is his growing attachment to insignificant things of the world, especially money. At first, money is to him a legitimate means to his desired end: Kamala's affections. But he soon masters the art of love, and ceases to make any sort of progress. Over the years he gradually grows more and more attached to money and finally this attachment becomes an obsession with him, driving out his former interest in, and compassion for, his fellow human beings. He ceases to be his own master; his own greed takes control over him and his "voice" is silenced.

The process is a very slow one. Whereas he quickly mastered the arts and the virtues of the Samanas and then moved on, he does not move on when he masters the arts of Kamala and Kamaswami, nor does he proceed to experience the art of the child-people, love. He remains in his rut and is gradually worn down by the meaninglessness of his life.

# SIDDHARTHA

## TEXTUAL ANALYSIS

## CHAPTER EIGHT: BY THE RIVER

........................................................

### TITLE

Siddhartha returns to the same river which he originally crossed some twenty years earlier. The river no longer marks a boundary between two different worlds. Siddhartha does not cross it now only to enter a new life, but he recognizes its values and he decides to remain "by" it.

### DESPAIR AND SUICIDE

Siddhartha reaches his lowest point as he looks into the river and contemplates suicide. As often in Hesse, despair is here presented as a necessary prelude to entering a state of heightened consciousness and happiness. Siddhartha's realization of the folly of his thoughts of suicide comes quickly. Although he has been out of touch with the concept of Perfection for many years, he nonetheless thinks of the holy word "Om" and finds new strength.

## CHARACTERIZATION

The reappearance of Govinda provides the opportunity for a new comparison of him and his old friend. Whereas Siddhartha has changed in every conceivable way during the time which has transpired since their last meeting-in keeping with his aim to experience the world, as well as in keeping with the nature of the World of the Mother-Govinda's face retains the same characteristics as before. He is loyal and eager, but also fearful. In brief, he has followed the teachings of Buddha, but has not progressed in any way.

Siddhartha suddenly makes a great leap forward. He is revitalized by his long sleep (perhaps suggesting contact with his unconscious and its healing effect), and has finally acquired at least a preliminary appreciation of the nature and value of love. His long years of Samsara have not been wasted after all. Without them he would not have been so completely drained that he felt despair and contemplated suicide. Freed of all other concerns, his unconscious restores to him his former awareness of Perfection, and in addition he finds that he can now accept many things which he previously could not. He now laughs at the world, and not with the bitter laughter which previously accompanied his losses at gambling.

## THE SECOND AWAKENING

Just as he felt an awakening of new forces within himself when he left the Samanas, now, too, Siddhartha feels that he is experiencing a rebirth. He realizes that it was necessary for him to degenerate slowly and lose his former strength, so that he could reach a new and higher awareness. He now sees only the essence of the World of the Mother: all life is transitory, yet there is a permanence in the cycles of life. The river reminds him of this - and he accordingly resolves to remain by it.

## STRUCTURE

Just as the fourth chapter forms a transition between Siddhartha's first two periods, so does the eighth chapter form a transition between the second and third periods of his life. During the first two-thirds of his life, Siddhartha has experienced the incomplete World of the Father and the imperfect World of the Mother. Now he is ready to effect the necessary synthesis.

# SIDDHARTHA

## TEXTUAL ANALYSIS

### CHAPTER NINE: THE FERRYMAN

#### TITLE

Significantly, Vasudeva's name is not used in the title. Gotama and Kamala were important individuals, representing and epitomizing two worlds with which Siddhartha had to become familiar. But now Siddhartha has progressed beyond this early stage of development. He no longer seeks individuality, but rather synthesis. Hence the general term "ferryman" is used in preference to Vasudeva's name. The general term has the further advantage of suggesting his connection with the river.

#### THE RIVER

This chapter is dominated by the river. Siddhartha and the river are like old friends who get to know one another again following a long period of separation. The wise Vasudeva recognizes that the river has "spoken" to Siddhartha, as indeed it has. The river has many messages, the most important of which is that there is no such thing as time. Because of its ubiquitous nature, it conveys this insight to Siddhartha, as it has done to Vasudeva and to a very few other especially sensitive and receptive people.

## THE SMILE

The second of the novel's most important symbols also figures prominently in this chapter, and is mentioned in close connection with the river. As Siddhartha continues to learn from the river, he begins to acquire the radiant smile which is characteristic of Vasudeva. The smile replaces words; the two friends are able to sense each other's emotions, and words become, for the most part, superfluous.

## KAMALA'S DEATH

The death of Kamala is one of the more enigmatic events in the entire novel. She leaves her former life to become a follower of Buddha, thereby forsaking the Mother-World, of which she was the epitome, in favor of the Father-World. As a result, she loses her uniqueness, for which Siddhartha expressed admiration. As Cirlot's *Dictionary of Symbols* observes, "There is a clear connection between the snake and the feminine principle," so it would seem that Kamala's death indicates a final return to her own way, that of the Mother. Her death is described at some length, which is appropriate since death is one aspect of the Mother.

This **episode** points up the transience of the world, but it also suggests permanence. Kamala leaves behind a son, and the Unity of existence is thereby indicated. So Siddhartha and the reader feel that death is part of the ultimate harmony of the world. Kamala is cremated on the same hill where Vasudeva's wife was cremated, thereby establishing a further link between transience and permanence. Siddhartha, moved by Kamala's death, listens to the river and is able to perceive its message, which he has just experienced: Unity. Siddhartha's reaction to the death of his former lover is an indication of his own growth. He is neither detached and callous nor excessively sorrowful and sentimental; he has begun to experience the true meaning of love.

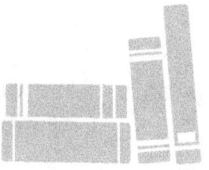

# SIDDHARTHA

## TEXTUAL ANALYSIS

### CHAPTER TEN: THE SON

**TITLE**

As in chapter nine, the generic term "son" is used in preference to the boy's name. His importance, like that of Vasudeva, does not lie in his individuality, but rather in his role. As a child, he suggests renewal and a form of permanence. He is also a final test for Siddhartha, who must overcome the strong, selfish attachment which he feels for the boy.

**LOVE AND THE CHILD-PEOPLE**

Siddhartha, reflecting on his condition, realizes that he has become like the child-people. He experiences love, a selfish love, just as they typically do. To be sure, Siddhartha does have altruistic, if misguided, reasons for not wishing the boy to leave; the has found peace, and foolishly believes that he can help his son arrive at the final stage of happiness more quickly. But a more important motivation is his purely selfish desire to hold on to his son at all costs. (This is reminiscent of the attitude of Tito's mother in *The Glass Bead Game*.)

Siddhartha realizes that he is experiencing a very unrefined kind of love. It is basically a form of attachment, yet it is also a strong and potentially noble emotion. It is a feeling which he never experienced before, even during the many years he spent among the child-people. This, too, is a necessary step, the final step, in Siddhartha's development. As Vasudeva points out, when Siddhartha manages to conquer this sense of attachment and learn to laugh, when he refines his love, he will have attained Perfection.

## THE GENERATIONS

There is a "generation gap" present in the novel. But the problems are much deeper. Siddhartha's final and most difficult task is to come to the realization that his son must be allowed to go his own way. The boy is "in the wrong." He should not repay his father's kindness with hostility; in general, he does not handle the situation as well as his father, "old" Siddhartha, did years previously. Young Siddhartha has learned none of the skills which his father had acquired at that age, and his road is bound to be a difficult one. Yet Siddhartha, too, is wrong. He sees only the irrelevant details and has lost sight of the essentials: an individual must be allowed to choose his own path, and everyone is bound to make many mistakes during the course of his life.

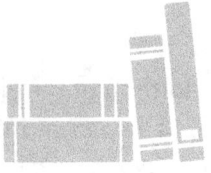

# SIDDHARTHA

## TEXTUAL ANALYSIS

## CHAPTER ELEVEN: OM

### TITLE

After years of searching, Siddhartha finally reaches his ultimate goal: "Om," Perfection.

### THE CHILD-PEOPLE

Siddhartha comes to feel more and more deeply his kinship with ordinary people, with the "child-people." He for the first time acquires the virtue of humility. He sees that he has one thing which they lack: awareness of the Unity of life. But they are perhaps superior to him in other respects: they partake more fully in the various aspects of human nature, such as love.

## THE RIVER

Once again the river is instrumental in helping Siddhartha come to an important realization. He hears it laugh at him, and realizes that he is acting foolishly. He sees his reflection in it and is reminded of his father. Then he suddenly knows that his son's departure is a repetition of his own decision to leave his home and his parents, and thereby is but another indication of the Unity of all things.

## SIDDHARTHA'S FINAL UNITY

Once again Siddhartha almost reaches the point of despair prior to making a leap forward. And once again he speaks at length to Vasudeva. The ferryman says very little, allowing his smile and the river to speak for him. Siddhartha listens, and for the first time hears the true, complete message of the river: "Om." His "wound" heals-he loses his selfish attachment to his son - and his Self merges into Unity.

## VASUDEVA'S DEATH

Vasudeva's death, unlike that of Kamala, is not described in the novel. The ferryman feels that his time has come and he walks out into the woods, into the Unity of all things. Kamala did not attain this unity. Her death served to restore her to her proper realm, that of the Mother, from which she had strayed, and hence it is painful. Vasudeva, on the other hand, is already at perfect harmony with the flow of events - and has been for years - so his death is merely a confirmation of his way of life. Accordingly, no violent break is suggested by the manner in which it is described by the narrator.

# SIDDHARTHA

## TEXTUAL ANALYSIS

### CHAPTER TWELVE: GOVINDA

**TITLE**

For the third and final time, an individual's name constitutes the title of a chapter. In this case, there are two implications. First, Siddhartha has attained Unity and can now accept Govinda's individuality without endangering his own development by becoming attached or subservient to him; and second, Govinda himself for the first time shows indications of emerging as an individual.

**WORDS**

Siddhartha here formulates his reasons for distrusting words. The very manner in which words express ideas invariably makes the expression one-sided, and therefore incomplete. Words, then, are at odds with the principle of the Unity of all things. This is one reason why teachings must be, in the end, inadequate; they are clothed in words and hence are incapable of expressing any truly noble sentiments or ideas.

## SIDDHARTHA AND GOTAMA

Siddhartha maintains that he now feels there to be no fundamental difference between his view and that of the Buddha. There is apparently one major, irreconcilable difference: Gotama forbids his followers to partake of earthly love, whereas Siddhartha feels that love is the most important thing in the world. In keeping with his low opinion of words, Siddhartha does not attempt to "explain" how he resolves the apparent contradiction within his own mind. But it is possible to read between the lines and offer a more detailed explanation of his attitude. Buddha, like Siddhartha, has attained a state in which he is capable of the highest form of unselfish love, Siddhartha now realizes. Yet Gotama forbids his followers to experience love. He must make this prohibition because he, in his avowed attempt to reduce the suffering of mankind, realizes that most people will remain entangled in selfish love if they do not eliminate love from their lives entirely. And a life without any attachments is preferable to a life ruled by them. Gotama's "system" is directed toward ordinary people, for whom a refined, selfless love-such as Siddhartha and Gotama himself ultimately attain-is an unrealistic goal.

## THE SMILE

Siddhartha's words have but little effect on his friend. Only when Govinda kisses Siddhartha (thereby indicating his readiness to experience the all-important emotion of love) and gazes into his face, does he feel the impact of Siddhartha's message. He sees

Unity, although he himself does not fully enter into this state of harmony.

## HESSE'S JUDGMENT OF HIS CHARACTERS

It is now possible to formulate, at least tentatively, Hesse's implicit judgment of the characters in *Siddhartha*. Gotama, Vasudeva, and Siddhartha are clearly the most perfect, most admirable characters in the book. Each is an individual who has found his own way to the desired goal of peace, harmony, and Unity.

Govinda and Kamala are on the whole quite admirable, but to some extent each lacks the qualities of the three figures discussed immediately above. Govinda does not possess the potential of his friend Siddhartha. He is a follower-to be sure, the best possible follower of the best teacher. But a follower cannot attain perfection, and only at the end does Govinda obtain a glimpse of the Unity in which Siddhartha fully shares.

Kamala, on the other hand, is a unique individual. The implicit comparison between her and the first woman encountered by Siddhartha points this out, and Siddhartha later comments upon it. But for some reason she becomes untrue to herself after once having found her own path. She was not meant to be a follower of the Buddha; the fact that she spoiled her son is a clear indication that she did not successfully adapt to her new way of life. She ultimately lacked the courage to face the approach of old age, and hence sought the illusion of permanence offered by the Father-World. Only on her deathbed does she return to the true path, her true path, the World of the Mother.

On a still lower level are the other people in the novel. Siddhartha's comment that the "child-people" are his equals cannot be taken at face value. His statement is a reflection of his newly acquired virtue of humility. It is a sincere, but inaccurate, assessment of the situation. Kamaswami, for example, is certainly judged unfavorably when the narrator compares him with Siddhartha and even with Kamala. Likewise, Siddhartha's father and the Samanas, as a group, lack the qualities which make Siddhartha, Gotama, and Vasudeva remarkable individuals.

The novel, then, represents a hierarchal system. Some men are simply portrayed as having more potential than others. A man who is born to be a "follower" must strive to be the best possible follower, but this is an inferior "calling" to the calling to be a trail-blazing, independent individual.

# SIDDHARTHA

## CHARACTER ANALYSES

### SIDDHARTHA

One of the names of the historical Buddha, Gotama, it signifies "the one who has attained his goal." There are certain similarities between Hesse's character in the novel and the historical figure, but the reader should be careful not to attempt to draw exact parallels.

Siddhartha is brought up in an ideal atmosphere; his parents provide the necessities - but not the luxuries-of life: love, guidance, and discipline. But he senses that their way is not his way and he rejects the path chosen for him by his father. He first spends some time with the Samanas, attempting to empty himself of all ties to the world-to transcend and overcome external reality, which he views with disdain. From the Buddha he learns that he does not have enough knowledge; that the road which he must follow is much more complicated than he previously realized. He therefore sets off on his own and he begins to correct his previous one-sided existence. Whereas he formerly attempted to eradicate the self, he now consciously and actively cultivates a heightened awareness of the self. He endeavors to expand his horizons by experiencing all that he can, and by becoming the master of all he undertakes. He realizes, both consciously and intuitively, that he must remain in control of himself and of his activities.

At first he is highly successful. He quickly masters the art of love and becomes a wealthy businessman. From the beginning, he is never subservient to Kamala or Kamaswami. He remains independent, while never failing to fulfill his obligations to them and to the other people he encounters. Business is merely a game for Siddhartha, a game which he does not take seriously. In fact, business is merely a means to attain Kamala's love, and to remain in her favor. He does feel committed to Kamala and to his relationship to her, which he highly values. But he does not "love" her, and he does not become her prisoner, or a prisoner of love.

Gradually Siddhartha comes to realize that a change is taking place within himself. Years pass, and he senses that he is no longer able to remain above his business activities. He begins to take them much too seriously, as Kamaswami has always done. He worries, drinks, gambles, and sees his former equanimity slipping away from him. He has grown attached to money, and to his way of life, while being less and less able to enjoy it. He becomes disgusted and departs, leaving behind him the one-sided world of the flesh just as he previously left behind the one-sided world of the spirit. Like many of Hesse's characters, including Emil Sinclair in *Demian* and Harry Haller in *Steppenwolf*, Siddhartha comes to realize that neither of the two polar opposites, nature and spirit, is sufficient-both must be experienced and understood, and in the end a kind of synthesis must be achieved.

Siddhartha intuitively follows a very "logical" and natural development. As a boy he devotes his energy to learning. He acquires the unusual skills of reading and writing, which are so useful to him later. More important, he learns to "think, to wait, and to fast." During the second period of his life, as a grown man in his prime years, he appropriately experiences life to the fullest, utilizing the self-discipline and skills which he acquired during his youth. Because of his experiences he comes closer to self-knowledge and self-fulfillment, and when he has derived all the benefit possible from his association with Kamala and Kamaswami, he retires to live a simple life of contemplation on the bank of the river with Vasudeva. Finally, as old age approaches, he attains the desired synthesis and the concomitant sense of equanimity. He experiences love, and with great effort manages to free himself from the dangerous sense of attachment which usually accompanies this most beautiful but most dangerous of emotions. Each step along the arduous road was a necessary one, and Siddhartha himself points out that even his lowest point-when he found himself on the brink of suicide-was a part of the development which he could not have done without. Siddhartha is independent and self-reliant from beginning to end. These admirable qualities make it possible for him to persevere and ultimately to achieve his goal.

## GOVINDA

The name means "keeper of cows," and hence suggests sanctity, since cows are sacred in Hindu philosophy. A great Hindu teacher by this name lived around 800 A.D., but no exact parallels exist between this man and the character in Hesse's novel.

Govinda, as portrayed by Hesse, is Siddhartha's boyhood friend and the two meet periodically in later life. Govinda is a good man, and a seeker of truth, but a person who lacks Siddhartha's extraordinary talents and sensitivity. The difference between the two is indicated early in the story when they both begin to practice meditation on a specific occasion. Govinda meditates only for the "customary time," whereupon he arises and is ready to leave. Siddhartha, on the other hand, loses contact with external reality and truly becomes lost in meditation.

Govinda is for the most part content to assume the role of a follower and disciple, first of Siddhartha, then of Gotama, the Buddha, and towards the conclusion of his life, once again of Siddhartha. He does not experience the extreme heights and depths of life as does Siddhartha, nor does he attain the same degree of insight into the universe and the Unity of things achieved by his friend.

## SIDDHARTHA'S FATHER

He is a good man, but one who is bound to the traditions of his Brahman religion. He expects Siddhartha to follow his way of life, and is very surprised when his son asks his permission to leave home. He does not understand why his son wants to leave, but he soon comes to realize that he must grant his permission.

## GOTAMA, THE BUDDHA

He was historically the last of the Buddhas (Buddha means "The Enlightened One"), and lived probably in the sixth century, B.C. The Gotama of the story, like his historical counterpart, is a holy man and a great teacher. He gives direction and guidance to many seekers of truth, like Govinda, who would be unable to define and attain their goal independently. He also serves as a model for Siddhartha, insofar as he is a great man who has found his own way to truth and fulfillment. Siddhartha learns from him, even though he does not follow his specific teachings.

## VASUDEVA

One of the names of Krishna, an incarnation of a Hindu deity it signifies "one in whom all things abide and who abides in all things." Vasudeva, the saintly ferryman, transports Siddhartha across the river when the latter sets out into the world after leaving the Buddha, and he later receives Siddhartha in his humble hut as a guest and then as a helper. Vasudeva lacks the sophistication of Siddhartha or Gotama, but he nonetheless attains a state of peace and fulfillment, and Siddhartha learns much from him-from his example and his smile, for the most part, rather than from his words. He is a good listener, and also helps Siddhartha in this role.

## KAMALA

The name is related to "Kama," the name of the Hindu god of love and desire; in its uncapitalized form, "kama" signifies physical love. Kamala is no ordinary courtesan, but is the very best of her kind. She is not only a highly skilled lover, but also has integrity and other qualities which contribute to her unique value as a human being. Siddhartha first sees her almost immediately after encountering a beautiful woman and rejecting her advances. Siddhartha must experience the ultimate in physical love in his quest for fulfillment, and only a woman with Kamala's qualities would be a suitable teacher and, later, an appropriate partner for him. The intensity of emotion felt by Siddhartha when Kamala dies is an indication that he has become more capable of experiencing the feelings of a genuine love than he was when he lived with her, and her death hence illustrates the progress made by Siddhartha in this important respect during the intervening eleven years. Kamala deserts her own way, that of the Mother, to become a follower of the Buddha. Her death marks her return to the World of the Mother.

## KAMASWAMI

The name comes from "Kama," which refers to the sensual and material pleasures of life, and "Swami," which means "Master." There seems to be irony in the name, since Kamaswami is certainly not the "Master" of the material pleasures of life, but is rather their slave. He teaches Siddhartha the elementary financial facts of the business world, but is completely unable to learn any of the more valuable lessons which Siddhartha could teach him.

## YOUNG SIDDHARTHA

The boy is hopelessly spoiled when he meets his father, and the two have nothing in common. In keeping with his nature, young Siddhartha runs away and does not seek his father's permission to leave. From his experience with the boy, Siddhartha first learns to love, and finally to overcome the selfish attachment of this love.

## THE CRITICS REACT TO SIDDHARTHA

There is probably more critical agreement regarding *Siddhartha* than any other of Hesse's works. It seems clear that the hero seeks and eventually attains Unity, so interpreters agree on the major **theme**. Furthermore, most critics like the work; they point out the unity of style and content, praising the structure of the book and the author's use of symbols.

The first major discussion of Hesse's *Siddhartha* is offered by Hugo Ball in his book *Hermann Hesse. Sein Leben und sein Werk* (1927; revised and expanded edition 1933). Ball admires greatly Hesse and his treatment of his subject is accordingly quite favorable. Ball stresses the Romantic aspect, and - unfortunately - calls Hesse "the last knight of Romanticism." His chapter on *Siddhartha* includes much background information which critics today often still rely upon, but his interpretation of the work has been superseded by more recent critical works.

One German dissertation on the novel has been published, *Lebensgestaltung und Weltanschauung in Hermann Hesse's* Siddhartha, by Johanna Kunze. This study consists primarily of a detailed discussion of the Indic background of the novel and analyzes the work in terms of Indian philosophy.

*Siddhartha* was one of the last of Hesse's major works to be translated into English. When it finally was published in America in 1951, the reaction was favorable, but muted. Few important reviews of the translation appeared, but they were for the most part favorable. One review, by Christopher Lazare in the *New York Times Book Review* of December 2, 1951, stresses Hesse's humanism and his anti-Nazi stance, and has little to say about the work itself outside of a brief plot summary. A second review, by Karl S. Weimar in the *German Quarterly*, vol. 26 (1953), p. 301, briefly praises the quality of the translation and observes that "only now can the English reader appreciate the unique coexistence of Eastern and Western philosophies in Hesse's work."

Only with the appearance of the article by Leroy Shaw in 1957 did serious discussion of *Siddhartha* begin in America. The books of Ziolkowski and Rose appeared in 1965, and books by Boulby and Field, as well as articles by Timpe, Butler, and others, followed.

It is unnecessary to discuss the English criticism of *Siddhartha* at length, since for the most part the various critics are in agreement. Most cite Hesse's long-standing interest in India, and in the process many quote from other of Hesse's works to support their conclusions. The mystical nature of *Siddhartha*'s goal seems clear, insofar as any mystical phenomenon can be called "clear," so there is little debate on this issue. It is universally recognized that the work contains elements of Hinduism, Buddhism, other Eastern philosophies, Christianity, Faust, Romanticism, and Hesse's own life. Students interested in a discussion of special problems in the work should consult the annotated bibliography at the conclusion of this study guide.

One notable exception to the above generalization is the article by Colin Butler, "Hermann Hesse's *Siddhartha*: Some Critical Objections." Butler vehemently attacks *Siddhartha* as poor literature, and his arguments deserve consideration. Basically Butler argues as follows:

In *Siddhartha*, "objective reality and wishful thinking" are confused so that the "way to peace of mind and the way to truth are presumed identical." In his search, Siddhartha is primarily motivated by a "gnawing anxiety which is the chief product of his sense of individuation, or his fear of death." Human relationships provide no comfort, so for lack of anything better he turns to a "new, solipsistic metaphysic."

Many objections to Butler's study can be raised. In the first place, he fails to grant Hesse the right to establish his own premises in his novel. *Siddhartha* is set in ancient India, and is by no stretch of the imagination a "realistic" novel. Of course, Siddhartha's specific resolution is incompatible with the world of 1970, but this is irrelevant. Siddhartha finds his own way at his own time, within his own given society, and that is what counts. Butler's explanation of Siddhartha's fear of death is likewise unfounded - the text of the novel simply does not confirm the assertion that a "gnawing fear of death" is of such importance to the hero. Butler's contention that Siddhartha has a "congenital inability to adapt to life" is likewise not true; on the contrary, Siddhartha adapts admirably to life's essentials, as he interprets them, within the context of his own society. Here Butler seems to fault Siddhartha for not being an "ordinary" person.

In brief, Butler attempts to force a "logical" interpretation upon a work which is ultimately religious and mystical. Thinking in Western terms, he maintains that Siddhartha cannot simultaneously possess a Self and have that Self merge into Unity. But the contradiction which Butler sees does not exist within the philosophical world of the novel. Many of his other objections (e.g., to Kamala's death and the son's departure) can be met by relating them to the important **themes** of the novel, such as the teacher-student (or father-son) relationship, and to the difference between the Worlds of the Father and the Mother.

# SIDDHARTHA

## ESSAY QUESTIONS AND MODEL ANSWERS

Question: On what basis can *Siddhartha* be appreciated as literature?

Answer: The world of *Siddhartha* is not realistic, but highly idealized; not rational, but mystical. The setting is distant and totally foreign. Accordingly, many modern readers may at first have difficulty accepting Siddhartha's single-minded pursuit of his abstract and undefined goal. The final vision is likewise "unbelievable," and may seem to reflect nothing more than an idealized fantasy world. It could furthermore be termed "insincere," since Hesse surely did not believe in this form of Eastern transfiguration. The style of the book may seem simplistic, and the internal structure, which reflects a division into three distinct sections, seems to be at odds with the external division into two unequal parts. Indeed, a case can be made for calling *Siddhartha* a very unsatisfactory work of literature!

In defense of the novel, it must first be pointed out that Hesse is working with an obviously unreal and symbolic world. A comparison with Goethe's *Faust* is helpful. Goethe no more believed in the devil or in a Christian heaven than Hesse believed in Buddhism or Hinduism, yet his Faust outwits the devil and is taken into heaven. Goethe, like Hesse, is saying, basically, that his hero has successfully completed his life within the given historical situation into which he is born. Nether rigidly follows his tradition; each searches for truth within the framework of his culture.

*Siddhartha* cannot be understood if it is approached rationally. Just as for Faust, in a Christian setting, heaven is the appropriate conclusion to a successful life, so is *Siddhartha*'s proper conclusion, in an ancient Indian setting, the attainment of a feeling of the Unity of all things. If this is accepted, the style and structure are seen to corroborate the **theme**. The style is simple and unified, and the overlapping double structure of four plus eight, and four plus four plus four chapters, suggests the unity of apparently separate entities.

Question: Is *Siddhartha* "relevant"?

Answer: The question must first be asked, "Relevant to what?" If the question primarily implies directly relevant to current social problems, then the answer must be no. The class structure of Indian society is scarcely mentioned, and certainly not criticized in any way in the novel. The author's attitude toward the financial situation in the novel likewise does not reflect a position which we would today call "relevant." Kamaswami is not favorably portrayed, but his wealth is not the reason. Siddhartha, a truly positive character, amasses huge sums of money in the midst of poverty, and is implicitly criticized only for having become attached to his wealth, not simply for having it.

On a more basic level, however, *Siddhartha* is indeed highly relevant. Siddhartha is true to himself, and accepts the given social conditions which at the time are not ready to be changed. Hesse's message is: Be true to yourself. Hesse would maintain that if it is followed rigorously, this credo (be it in the India of 800 B.C. or in America today) will lead to the best possible understanding of the relationship between the individual and the world around him, and with the aid of this understanding he will best be able to determine the specific actions appropriate for him in his specific situation.

Question: Discuss the relation of *Siddhartha* to Hesse's other works.

Answer: At first glance, *Siddhartha* may seem to be quite different from Hesse's other novels. Yet it has much in common with most of Hesse's works. Here, as always, symbols play an extremely important role and are, in fact, of greater significance than the actual "plot" or action of the story. The problem of the polarity between the Worlds of the Father and the Mother is likewise a feature common to many of Hesse's novels, including *Siddhartha*. Apparently insignificant details often have symbolic value based on this polarity. Most significantly, the central **theme** of the novel, the hero's quest for self-fulfillment, is found in all of Hesse's important works. Siddhartha, like Emil Sinclair, Harry Haller, Goldmund, H.H., and Joseph Knecht, comes to realize that his original conception of the nature of life was inadequate or incomplete.

To be sure, Siddhartha alone among the leading characters completely and unambiguously achieves his goal. But this is really not a significant difference. It is more a reflection of the idealized setting of *Siddhartha* than of the hero's greater achievement. Siddhartha's final state of transfiguration is modeled on - but is by no means identical to - the state of Nirvana, which actually exists within the Indian system in which the action of the novel takes place. That Siddhartha achieves a more perfect synthesis of all aspects of life than any of Hesse's other characters is, then, basically a reflection of the simplicity of his society.

Question: Could *Siddhartha* be called a Buddhistic, Hindu, or Christian work?

Answer: Elements of all three religions can be detected in the work, and Hesse readily admitted that he was concerned with each of them. Externally, the influence of Buddhism seems most prominent. The names Siddhartha and Gotama refer to the historical Buddha, and his Four Noble Truths and Eight fold Path are alluded to in the course of the novel. Parallels can be drawn between Siddhartha and the historical Gotama. At the end of the novel, Siddhartha says that he sees no real difference between his own ultimate position and that of the Buddha.

External, in less obvious, parallels to Hinduism can also be drawn. The names Vasudeva and Govinda allude to aspects of this religion and the Hindu Bhagavad-Gita seems to have influenced the composition of *Siddhartha*. The most significant parallel, however, is to be found in the similarity of the nature of the quest in the novel and in the Hindu religion. Siddhartha's goal remains undefined, as does the Hindu's goal.

Christian elements can also be detected. The emphasis on love in Siddhartha's formulation of his final state of transcendence is Christian, as Hesse himself has pointed out. Elements of a specific Protestant Christianity-reluctance to accept the rituals and dogma of the father's religion, and the hero's insistence upon interpreting and defining his own relation to the Absolute - are present too.

There are, then, elements of all three religion, and, indeed of many other "religious" prophets from Lao-tse to Nietzsche. And this mingling of philosophies corresponds to the **theme** of the book: the greatest of men, such as Buddha and Jesus, found a way which was right for them; their way may also be right for others, but this will not necessarily be the case - and it is certainly not the case for Siddhartha, who feels compelled to find his own unique path to self-fulfillment.

# BIBLIOGRAPHY

## ENGLISH EDITIONS

*Knulp. Three Tales from the Life of Knulp*, translated by Ralph Mannheim. New York: Farrar, Straus and Giroux, 1971. This good, reliable translation is now available as a Noonday paperback.

*Klingsor's Last Summer*, translated by Richard and Clara Winston. New York: Farrar, Straus and Giroux, 1970; now available as a Noonday paperback. A good, reliable translation (the student should, however, be aware that the style of the title story makes it extremely difficult to render into English).

## BOOKS ON HESSE'S LIFE AND WORKS

Most of the recent criticism on Hesse has been done in English by North American scholars. Eight books are readily available to the student. The first, *Hermann Hesse and His Critics. The Criticism and Bibliography of Half a Century* (Chapel Hill, N.C.: University of North Carolina Press, 1958), by Joseph Mileck, contains a concise survey of Hesse's life and works followed by a detailed annotated bibliography. Excellent summaries of the contents of all important criticism of Hesse prior to 1957 can be found in this valuable book.

The first comprehensive survey of Hesse in English was *Faith from the Abyss: Hermann Hesse's Way from Romanticism to Modernity* (New York: New York University Press, 1965; now available in paperback), by Ernst Rose. This book contains detailed summaries, with quotations, of most of Hesse's works, including the early novels and the major short stories. The book is, however, too short to do justice to the subject and hence often tends to be superficial. Rose's treatment of the stories discussed in this study guide is more detailed than that of most other interpreters.

The first significant original study to appear in English was Theodore Ziolkowski's *The Novels of Hermann Hesse. A Study in **Theme** and Structure* (Princeton University Press, 1965; now available in paperback). This excellent book offers detailed interpretations of the major novels, beginning with *Demian*, as well as separate preliminary discussions of several of Hesse's major themes, including "Magical Thinking," "Timelessness," and "Humor." It closes with a discussion of Hesse's position between Romanticism and Existentialism. Ziolkowski often refers to Hesse's untranslated essays and letters to support his interpretations, thereby offering the American reader insights into important aspects of Hesse's thought which would otherwise be inaccessible. He also stresses connections between Hesse and other writers. Of particular interest is Ziolkowski's discussion of the symbolism of *Demian* and the structure of *Steppenwolf*. In his opinion, *Narcissus and Goldmund* is Hesse's least successful novel. The short stories are not treated individually.

Also by Ziolkowski, the pamphlet "Hermann Hesse" (New York: Columbia University Press Paperback, 1966), offers a good introduction to the author and can be highly recommended. The short stories are dealt with briefly, but effectively.

A very comprehensive survey of Hesse is offered in Mark Boulby's *Hermann Hesse. His Mind and Art* (Ithaca: Cornell University Press, 1967). Most of Hesse's important prose is discussed here. Although the emphasis remains on the major novels, two early works, *Peter Camenzind* and *Beneath the Wheel*, also receive in-depth treatment. The interpretations are invariably balanced and convincing. Frequent references to minor works help form a well-rounded picture of Hesse. The book has an excellent index and with its help the reader can easily locate a discussion of important concepts and symbols in Hesse's works. Sections on the short stories are short but valuable.

An excellent book is *Hermann Hesse* (New York: Twayne, 1970; now available in paperback), by George W. Field, the only complete, systematic survey of Hesse's life and works available in English. Since it covers Hesse's entire career, it does not discuss the major works in as much depth as do Ziolkowski and Boulby. The book has an extensive bibliography of books and articles on Hesse. A particularly valuable chapter is devoted to Hesse's poetry and non-fictional prose. The treatment of *Klingsor's Last Summer* is detailed; *Knulp* is not discussed in depth.

The most recent survey to appear in English is Bernhard Zeller, *Portrait of Hesse: An Illustrated Biography*, translated by Mark Hollebone (New York: Herder and Herder, 1971). This book is of significantly less value than the other books on Hesse discussed above. It is a rather unreliable abridgment of a documentary biography originally written in German. The illustrations, however, will be of interest to many readers.

Finally, *The Impact of Nietzsche on Hermann Hesse*, a short study by Herbert W. Reichert (Mt. Pleasant, Michigan: The Enigma Press, 1972) can be recommended as a useful introduction to a complex topic. Nietzschean aspects of *Klingsor's Last Summer* are considered by Reichert.

Two books in German deserve mention. *Hermann Hesse. Sein Leben und sein Werk* by Hugo Ball (new edition, updated by Anni Carlsson and Otto Basler, Zurich: Fretz & Wasmuth, 1947); this study, which originally appeared in 1927, was the first important book on Hesse and has been very influential. *Hermann Hesse. Natur und Geist*, by Hans Jurg Luthi (Stuttgart: Kohlhammer, 1970), is the latest major study of Hesse by a European.

The only important article on the short stories discussed in this study guide is Heinz W. Puppe, "Psychologie und Mystik in 'Klein and Wagner' von Hermann Hesse," *PMLA*, Vol. 78, pp. 28-35, 1963. A detailed discussion of Puppe's argument is given above, in the section on "Klein and Wagner."

## ARTICLES OF INTEREST TO READERS OF HESSE'S SHORT STORIES

The following articles are of particular interest, although not all deal explicitly with the short stories. All are written in English, but some, marked by an asterisk, quote from Hesse in the original German.

Benn, Maurice. "An Interpretation of the Work of Hermann Hesse." *German Life and Letters*, Vol. 3, pp. 202-211, 1949-50. Good general discussion of Hesse's main works, stressing the Nature-Spirit dichotomy.

*Brunner, John W. "The Natur-Geist [Nature-Spirit, i.e., Mother-Father] Polarity in Hermann Hesse." Helen Adolf Festschrift, ed. Sheema Buehne, et. al. New York: Ungar, pp. 268-484, 1968. A survey of this important concept in all of Hesse's works.

Butler, Colin. "Literary Malpractice in Some Works of Hermann Hesse." *University of Toronto Quarterly*, Vol. 40, pp. 168-82, 1971. An extremely critical general study; questions Hesse's capabilities as a writer.

Colby, Thomas E. "The Impenitent Prodigal: Hermann Hesse's Hero." *The German Quarterly*, Vol. 40, pp. 14-23, 1967. Sees Hesse's major **protagonist** as Prodigal Sons who fail to return to the Father (i.e., to traditional authority).

Engel, Eva J. "Hermann Hesse," in *German Men of Letters*, Vol. 2, pp. 249-274. London: O. Wolff, 1963. An introductory survey.

Fickert, Kurt J. "The Development of the Outsider Concept In Hesse's Novels." *Monatshefte*, Vol. 52, pp. 171-178, 1960. The conflict between the individual and society as reflected in Hesse's heroes.

Koester, Rudolf. "Self-Realization: Hesse's Reflections on Youth." *Monatshefte*, Vol. 58, pp. 181-186, 1965. Hesse's treatment of youth and the struggle for identity.

Naumann, Walter "The Individual and Society in the Work of Hermann Hesse." *Monatshefte*, Vol. 41, pp. 33-42, 1949. A perceptive discussion of one of the most important problems in Hesse's works.

Otten, Anna. (Editor) *Hesse Companion*. Frankfort: Suhrkamp, 1970. The editor gives a good survey of Hesse's works, which is followed by chapters on Hesse, for the most part reprinted from other important studies of Hesse. The *Hesse Companion* also offers a sample of critical commentary on Hesse- for the most part favorable - and contains a vocabulary and glossary for the benefit of students who wish to consult the original German of some of Hesse's works. It also contains an extensive bibliography. In short: a very valuable book, although none of the chapters specifically deals with the short stories.

Schwarz, Egon. "Hermann Hesse, the American Youth Movement, and Problems of Literary Evaluation." *PMLA*, Vol. 85, 1970, pp. 977-987. Discussion of Hesse's popularity in America and Germany, within the context of the more general problem of literary evaluation.

Seidlin, Oskar. "Hermann Hesse. The Exorcism of the Demon." *Symposium*, Vol. 4, 1950, pp. 325-348 (reprinted in O. Seidlin, *Essays in German and Comparative Literature*, Chapel Hill: University of North Carolina Press, 1961). An early, but still valuable study of several key **themes** in Hesse's writings.

Timpe, Eugene F. "Hermann Hesse in the United States." *Symposium*, Vol. 23, pp. 73-79, 1969,. An account of Hesse's popularity in America, concentrating as much on his early lack of popularity as on his later emergence as a cult figure.

Wilson, Colin. *The Outsider*. London: Victor Gollancz, 1956. The classic study of the Outsider **theme**. Wilson's appreciative treatment of Hesse's outsider figures contributed greatly toward increasing Hesse's popularity in the United States.

Ziolkowski, Theodore. "Saint Hesse among the Hippies." *American German Review*, Vol. 35, No. 2, pp. 18-23, 1969. The best short description of Hesse's current popularity.

## ANNOTATED BIBLIOGRAPHY

### English edition

*Siddhartha*, translated by Hilda Rosner. New York: New Directions, 1951: reprinted many times as a paperback. In general, a reliable translation.

### Books on Hesse's life and works

Most of the recent criticism on Hesse has been done in English by North American scholars. Six books are readily available to the student. The first, *Hermann Hesse and His Critics. The Criticism and Bibliography of Half a Century* (Chapel Hill, N.C.: University of North Carolina Press, 1958), by Joseph Mileck, contains a concise survey of Hesse's life and works followed by a detailed annotated bibliography. Excellent summaries of the contents of all important criticism of Hesse prior to 1957 can be found in this valuable book.

The first comprehensive survey of Hesse in English was *Faith from the Abyss: Herman Hesse's Way from Romanticism to Modernity* (New York: New York University Press, 1965; now available in paperback), by Ernst Rose. This book contains detailed summaries, with quotations, of most of Hesse's works, including the early novels and the major short stories. The book is, however, too short to do justice to the subject and hence often tends to be superficial. The chapter on *Siddhartha*, which stresses parallels with Christianity, Hinduism, and Lao-Tse, can be read with profit.

The first significant original study to appear in English was Theodore Ziolkowski's *The Novels of Hermann Hesse. A Study in **Theme** and Structure* (Princeton University Press, 1965; now available in paperback). This excellent book offers detailed interpretations of the major novels, beginning with *Demian*, as well as separate preliminary discussions of several of Hesse's major themes, including "Magical Thinking," "Timelessness," and "Humor." It closes with a discussion of Hesse's position between Romanticism and Existentialism. Ziolkowski often refers to Hesse's untranslated short stories and letters to support his interpretations, thereby offering the American reader insights into important aspects of Hesse's thought which would otherwise be inaccessible. He also stresses connections between Hesse and other writers. Of particular interest are Ziolkowski's discussion of the symbolism of *Demian* and the structure of *Steppenwolf*. In his opinion, *Narcissus and Goldmund* is Hesse's least successful novel. The long chapter on *Siddhartha* is especially valuable for its discussion of the structure and the major symbols (the river, the smile).

Also by Ziolkowski, the pamphlet "Hermann Hesse" (New York: Columbia University Paperback, 1966), offers a good introduction to the author and can be highly recommended.

A very comprehensive survey of Hesse is offered in Mark Boulby's *Hermann Hesse. His Mind and Art* (Ithaca: Cornell University Press, 1967). Most of Hesse's important prose is discussed here. Although the emphasis remains on the major novels, two early works, *Peter Camenzind* and *Beneath the Wheel*, also receive in-depth treatment. The interpretations are invariably balanced and convincing. The frequent references to minor works help form a well-rounded picture of Hesse. The book has an excellent index and with its help the reader can easily locate a discussion of important concepts and symbols in Hesse's works. The chapter on *Siddhartha* measures up to the author's usual high standards.

The most recent book, *Hermann Hesse* (New York: Twayne, 1970; now available in paperback), by George W. Field, is the only complete, systematic survey of Hesse's life and works. Since it covers Hesse's entire career, it does not discuss the major works in as much depth as do Ziolkowski and Boulby. But Field does discuss certain aspects of each of the major novels and often adds new perspectives. The book has an extensive bibliography of books and articles on Hesse. A particularly valuable chapter is devoted to Hesse's poetry and non-fictional prose. *Siddhartha* is discussed together with other of Hesse's stories from the same period and, as usual, provides valuable background information.

## Articles of interest to readers of *Siddhartha*

The following articles are of particular interest. All are written in English, but some, marked by an asterisk, quote from Hesse in the original German.

Beerman, Hans. "Hermann Hesse and the Bhagavad-Gita." *The Midwest Quarterly*, Vol. 1, pp. 27-40, 1959. An introductory essay on this important topic. Should be read in conjunction with the more detailed analysis of Eugene F. Timple.

*Butler, Colin. "Hermann Hesse's *Siddhartha*; Some Critical Objections." *Monatshefte*, Vol. 63, pp. 117-124, 1971. A violent polemic against Hesse's work; see the detailed analysis above.

_____, "Literary Malpractice in Some Works of Hermann Hesse." *University of Toronto Quarterly*, Vol. 40, pp. 168-82, 1971. An extremely critical, general study; questions Hesse's capabilities as a writer.

*Brunner, John W. "The Natur-Geist [Nature-Spirit, i.e., Mother-Father] Polarity in Hermann Hesse." Helen Adolf Festschrift, ed. Sheema Buehne, et. al. New York: Ungar, 1968, pp. 268-284. A survey of this important concept in all of Hesse's works. Brunner concludes that *Siddhartha* is the only work "in which Hesse successfully blended both into the experience of a single person."

Engel, Eva. "Hermann Hesse." *German Men of Letters*, Vol. 2. London: O. Wolff, 1963, pp. 249-274. A general survey.

*Hughes, Kenneth. "Hesse's Use of Gilgamesh-Motifs in the Humanization of Siddhartha and Harry Haller." *Seminar*, Vol. 5, pp. 129-140, 1969. An interesting study of literary relationships.

Mishra, Bhabagrahi. "An Analysis of Indic Tradition in Hermann Hesse's Siddhartha." *Indian Literature*, Vol. 11, pp. 111-123, 1968. An elementary and rather superficial survey which draws heavily upon Ziolkowski's interpretation. It includes a fairly detailed account of Hesse's interest in India.

Otten, Anna. (Editor) *Hesse Companion*. Frankfort: Suhrkamp, 1970. The editor gives a good survey of Hesse's works, which is followed by chapters on Hesse, for the most part reprinted from other important studies of Hesse. The *Hesse Companion* also offers a sample of critical commentary on Hesse-for the most part favorable - and contains a vocabulary and glossary for the benefit of students who wish to consult the original German of some of Hesse's works. It also contains an extensive bibliography. In short: a very valuable book. The interpretation of *Siddhartha* is taken from Ziolkowski's book.

Schludermann, Brigitte, and Rosemarie Finlay. "Mythical Reflections of the East in Hermann Hesse." *Mosaic*, Vol. 2, Nr. 3. pp. 97-111, 1968/69. A thematic study of an important problem in Hesse.

Schwarz, Egon. "Hermann Hesse, the American Youth Movement, and Problems of Literary Evaluation." *PMLA*, Vol. 85, pp. 977-987, 1970. Discussion of Hesse's popularity in America and Germany, within the context of the more general problem of literary evaluation.

Seidlin, Oskar. "Hermann Hesse. The Exorcism of the Demon." *Symposium*, Vol. 4, pp. 325-348, 1950 (reprinted in O. Seidlin, *Essays in German and Comparative Literature*, Chapel Hill: University of North Carolina Press, 1961). An early, but still valuable study of several key **themes** in Hesse's writings.

Shaw, Leroy R. "Time and the Structure of Hermann Hesse's *Siddhartha*." *Symposium*, Vol. 11, pp. 204-224, 1957. A well-written scholarly interpretation. Much of the argument is based upon the assumption that the division of the work into two parts of four and eight chapters corresponds to Siddhartha's encounter with the Four Noble Truths and Eightfold Path of Buddha. In spite of Theodore Ziolkowski's convincing refutation of this aspect of Shaw's interpretation, his article contains much valuable information and is definitely of interest to the student of *Siddhartha*.

Timpe, Eugene F. "Hermann Hesse in the United States." *Symposium*, Vol. 23, pp. 73-79, 1969. An account of Hesse's popularity in America, concentrating as much on his early lack of popularity as on his emergence as a cult figure.

*____; "Hesse's *Siddhartha* and the Bhagavad Gita." *Comparative Literature*, Vol. 22, pp. 346-57, 1970. A scholarly interpretation which analyzes in depth the relationship between Hesse and Hinduism.

Zeller, Bernhard. *Portrait of Hesse: An Illustrated Biography*. Translated by Mark Hollebone. New York: Herder and Herder, 1971. Although this is a book, and not an article, it is included in this section because it is of significantly less value than the other books on Hesse discussed above. It is a rather unreliable abridgement of a documentary biography originally written in German.

Ziolkowski, Theodore. "Saint Hesse among the Hippies." *American German Review*, Vol. 35, No. 2, pp. 18-23, 1969. The best short description of Hesse's current popularity.

## Suggested related reading: primary sources

*Buddhist Texts Through the Ages*. Edited by Edward Conze. Oxford: Oxford University Press, 1954.

*The Bhagavad-Gita: The Song of God*. Translated by Swami Prabhavanda and Christopher Isherwood. New York; Harper, 1951.

*The Upanishads*. Translated by Swami Nikilananda. Four volumes. New York: Harper, 1959.

## Suggested related reading: secondary sources

Coomaraswamy, Ananda K. *Hinduism and Buddhism*. New York: Philosophical Library, 1959.

Fingesten, Peter. *East is East. Hinduism, Buddhism, Christianity: A Comparison*. Philadelphia: Muhlenberg Press, 1956

Organ, Troy Wilson. *The Hindu Quest for the Perfection of Man*. Athens, Ohio: Ohio University, 1970.

Ross, Floyd H. *The Meaning of Life in Hinduism and Buddhism*. London: Routledge and Kegan Paul, 1952.

Weber, Max. *The Religion of India: The Sociology of Hinduism and Buddhism*. Translated by Hans H. Gerth and Don Martindale. New York: The Free Press, 1958. By an eminent German sociologist who was older than Hesse; the original German edition appeared prior to *Siddhartha*.

# SIDDHARTHA

## TOPICS FOR RESEARCH AND CRITICISM

..................................................

### THEMES AND TECHNIQUES OF *SIDDHARTHA*

*Siddhartha*: A lyrical novel?

> The Structure of *Siddhartha*
>
> The role of teachers in *Siddhartha*
>
> Hesse's affirmation of life in *Siddhartha*
>
> Self-fulfillment: A comparison of the major characters
>
> *Siddhartha* and its appeal to today's youth

### BACKGROUND AND SOURCES OF THE NOVEL

*Siddhartha* and German Romanticism

> *Siddhartha* and the "Bildungsroman" ("Novel of Education")

*Siddhartha* and the historical Buddha: biographical parallels and their significance

Dreams in *Siddhartha*: Jungian or Freudian?

*Siddhartha* and Buddism

*Siddhartha* and Hinduism

*Siddhartha* and Lao-tse

*Siddhartha* and Christian Protestantism

Elements of Nietzschean thought in *Siddhartha*

## HESSE'S CHARACTERIZATION

The nature of Govinda's final vision

Siddhartha, his father, and his son: A three-way comparison

Hesse's portrayal of women in *Siddhartha*

The "child-people"

Gotama and Vasudeva: A comparison

Siddhartha and Kamaswami as businessmen

## *SIDDHARTHA* AND HESSE'S OTHER WORKS

The woman as teacher in Hesse: Kamala and Hermine

"Teachers and teachers": Max Demian and Gotama

The "generation gap" in Hesse

Water **imagery** in *Siddhartha*, *Narcissus and Goldmund*, and *The Glass Bead Game*

The smile in *Siddhartha*, *The Glass Bead Game*, and *Journey to the East*

The "East" in *Siddhartha* and *Journey to the East*

Death in Hesse: An analysis based upon Kamala, Vasudeva, Max Demian, Goldmund, and Joseph Knecht

The triadic rhythm in Hesse's works

The concluding vision of *Siddhartha* and *Journey to the East*: A comparison

The beatific smile of Siddhartha and the laughter of the Immortals in *Steppenwolf*

Siddhartha and Goldmund

Love in *Siddhartha* and *The Glass Bead Game*

Friendship in *Siddhartha* and *Narcissus and Goldmund*

Patience in *Siddhartha* and *Journey to the East*

Discipline in *Siddhartha* and *Demian*

## COMPARISONS WITH OTHER WRITERS

(Note: *Siddhartha* is far from typical modern literature. Most of the suggested topics here will accordingly be contrastive in nature.)

*Siddhartha* and Nietzsche's "Will to Power"

Love in *Siddhartha* and in R.M. Rilke's *The Notebooks of Malte Laurids Brigge*

*Siddhartha* and Goethe's *Faust*

Two products of 1922: *Siddhartha* and Eliot's *Waste Land*

*Siddhartha* and Saul Bellow's *Henderson the Rain King*: Two conceptions of the Quest

The river in *Siddhartha* and in Thomas Wolfe's *Of Time and the River*

## POINTS OF CONTENTION AMONG THE CRITICS

Colin Butler's assessment of Hesse: Right or wrong?

The Four Noble Truths and the Eightfold Path: An assessment of the arguments of Shaw and Ziolkowski

www.ingramcontent.com/pod-product-compliance
Lightning Source LLC
LaVergne TN
LVHW011728060526
838200LV00051B/3073